KITCHEN FAVOURITES

Over **120** recipes from our most-loved chefs

EBURY
PRESS

1 3 5 7 9 10 8 6 4 2

Ebury Press, an imprint of Ebury Publishing,

20 Vauxhall Bridge Road,

London SW1V 2SA

Ebury Press is part of the Penguin Random House group of companies

whose addresses can be found at global.penguinrandomhouse.com

All texts and recipes on pages 9, 38, 65, 69, 74, 112, 119, 123, 128 © Rick Stein 2011; pages 10, 17, 21, 25, 42, 50, 57, 62, 73, 82, 86, 115, 120, 124, 135, 144, 155, 160, 171, 188 © Ken Hom 2012; pages 13, 14, 33, 37, 46, 61, 85, 90, 102, 139, 143, 147, 168, 172, 179, 202, 210, 221, 230 © Gizzi Erskine 2012; pages 18, 30, 34, 54, 78, 81, 97, 127, 132, 140, 148, 152, 163, 167, 184, 193, 201, 206, 217, 222, 226, 229, 234 © Ainsley Harriott 2011; pages 22, 26, 89, 98, 105, 116, 156, 164, 175, 180, 187 © Antonio Carluccio 2011; pages 29, 45, 53, 70, 77, 94, 101, 106, 131, 136, 151, 159, 176, 183 © Madhur Jaffrey 2011; pages 41, 49, 66, 93, 111, 198, 209, 213, 218, 233, 249 © Raymond Blanc 2012; pages 194, 197, 205, 214, 225, 237, 238, 241, 242, 245, 246, 250, 253, 254, 257, 258, 261, 262, 265, 266 © Mary Berry 2011.

All recipes in this book have previously appeared in the My Kitchen Table series previously published by Ebury Press.

Photographs on page 39 © Earl Carter; page 264 © Jean Cazals; pages 11, 16, 20, 24, 43, 51, 56, 63, 67, 83, 87, 92, 114, 121, 125, 154, 189, 208, 219 © Jean Cazals 2000, 2002 and 2003; pages 40, 48, 110, 199, 212, 232, 248 © Jean Cazals, Woodland Books Ltd 2012; pages 19, 55, 126, 162 © Gus Filgate, Woodland Books Ltd 2011; pages 256, 259, 260 © Dan Jones; pages 80, 228 © Dan Jones, Woodland Books Ltd 2011; pages 47, 60, 203, 211, 220 © David Loftus; pages 64, 113, 122, 129 © James Murphy; pages 84, 173, 231 © Ian O'Leary; pages 79, 149, 153, 166, 192, 207, 223, 227 © Juliet Piddington, Woodland Books Ltd 2011; pages 12, 15, 32, 36, 91, 103, 138, 142, 146, 169, 178 © William Reavel, Virgin Books 2012; pages 195, 204, 224, 236, 239, 240, 243, 244, 247, 251, 252, 255, 263, 267 © William Reavell © Woodland Books Ltd; pages 8, 23, 27, 68, 75, 88, 99, 104,117, 118, 157, 165, 174, 181, 186 © William Reavell, Woodland Books Ltd 2011; pages 145, 161, 170 © William Reavell, Woodland Books Ltd 2012; page 107 © Craig Robertson; pages 35, 96, 141, 185, 216 © Howard Shooter, Woodland Books Ltd 2011; pages 28, 44, 52, 71, 76, 95, 100, 130, 137, 150, 158, 177, 182 © Yuki Sigiura, Ebury Press; pages 196, 215 © Philip Webb, Woodland Books Ltd; pages 72, 134 © Philip Webb, Woodland Books Ltd 1996; pages 31, 133, 200, 235 Francesca Yorke Photography © Woodland Books Ltd 2011.

This compilation first published for WHSmith by Ebury Press in 2017

www.eburypublishing.co.uk

A CIP catalogue record for this book is available from the British Library

ISBN 9781785037290

WHSmith will donate £2 from the sale of each copy of *Kitchen Favourites* to Cancer Research UK, in support of the Stand Up To Cancer campaign.

Stand Up To Cancer and Stand Up To Cancer brand marks are registered trademarks or trademarks of the Entertainment Industry Foundation. Cancer Research UK is a registered charity in England & Wales (No. 1089464), Scotland (No. SC041666) and Isle of Man (1103)

Printed and bound in China by Leo Paper Products Ltd

Contents

FOREWORD

This year WHSmith celebrates its 225th anniversary. To mark this momentous occasion, we are pledging to raise £2 million to donate to our chosen charities.

WHSmith would like to thank everyone involved in the creation of this wonderful cookbook that offers over 120 delicious recipes from our favourite chefs. The book includes a selection of soups and starters, light bites and lunches, simple suppers and sweet treats and puds, so there is something for everyone.

For every copy of the book we sell, we will donate £2 to Stand Up To Cancer. One hundred per cent of all donations to Stand Up To Cancer go directly to fund game-changing cancer treatments. This translational research enables Cancer Research UK to speed up the process of turning discoveries in the labs into treatments for patients, which means more lives can be saved.

Sandra Bradley
WHSmith Books Team

SOUPS
AND
STARTERS

Rick Stein's

CRAB AND SWEETCORN SOUP

INGREDIENTS

1.2 litres (2 pints) good-quality chicken
    stock
2 fresh corn cobs
225g (8oz) fresh white crabmeat
5 tsp cornflour
1 tsp very finely chopped fresh ginger
2 spring onions, cut into 2.5cm (1in) pieces
    and finely shredded lengthways
1 tbsp light soy sauce
1 tbsp Chinese rice wine or dry sherry
1 egg white, lightly beaten
salt and freshly ground black pepper

This is the first oriental dish I ever ate at a Chinese restaurant, in Peterborough, England, in 1964, and it is a world classic that is so often ruined by sickly sweet tins of creamed corn, tasteless crab and gloopy cornflour. I thought it would be interesting to restore the dish to its simplicity and reliance on good, fresh ingredients.

1. Bring the chicken stock to the boil in a pan. Meanwhile, stand the corn cobs up on a board and slice away the kernels with a large sharp knife. Add the corn to the stock and simmer for 5 minutes.

2. Check over the crabmeat for any little pieces of shell, keeping the meat in the largest pieces possible. Mix the cornflour to a smooth paste with a little cold water, stir it into the soup and simmer for 2 minutes.

3. Stir in the crabmeat, ginger, spring onions, soy sauce, rice wine or sherry, 1 teaspoon of salt and some pepper to taste. Simmer for 1 minute.

4. Now give the soup a good stir, remove the spoon and slowly trickle in the beaten egg white so that it forms long, thin strands in the soup. Simmer for about 30 seconds and then serve immediately.

Ken Hom's

CLASSIC CHINESE CHICKEN STOCK

INGREDIENTS

2kg (4½lb) raw chicken feet, wings, etc., or any leftover bones you may have (save uncooked chicken bones and keep them in the freezer until you need them)

675g (1½lb) chicken pieces, such as wings, thighs, drumsticks

5 litres (8 pints) cold water

3 slices fresh ginger, cut on the diagonal into 5 × 1cm (2 × ½in) slices

6 spring onions, green tops removed

6 garlic cloves, unpeeled, but lightly crushed

1 tsp salt

Your first step on the path to success with Chinese cooking is to prepare and maintain an ample supply of good chicken stock. I prefer to make a large amount and freeze it. Once you have a batch of stock available you will be able to prepare any number of soups or sauces very quickly.

1. Put all the chicken into a very large pot (the bones can be put in either frozen or defrosted). Cover with the cold water and bring to a simmer.

2. Using a large, shallow spoon, skim off the scum as it rises from the bones to the surface of the water. Watch the heat, as the stock should never boil. Keep skimming as necessary until the stock looks clear. This can take 20–40 minutes at a low simmer. Do not stir or disturb the stock.

3. Now add the ginger, spring onions, garlic cloves and salt. Simmer the stock over a very low heat for 2–4 hours, skimming any fat off the top at least twice. The stock should be rich and full-bodied, which is why it needs to be simmered for such a long time.

4. Strain the stock through several layers of dampened muslin or through a very fine sieve. Let it cool thoroughly, then chill. Remove any fat that has risen to the top. It is now ready to be used or transferred to containers and frozen for future use.

Gizzi Erskine's

MEXICAN CHICKEN TORTILLA SOUP

INGREDIENTS

3 tbsp olive oil
2 onions, finely chopped
4 garlic cloves, finely chopped
2 red or green chillies, de-seeded and
   chopped
3 ripe tomatoes, chopped
900ml (1½ pints) chicken stock
1 × 275g (10oz) tin sweetcorn, drained
2 chicken breasts, skinned
sea salt and freshly ground black pepper

FOR THE TOPPING

2 medium (20cm/8in) flour tortillas, cut in
   half then thinly sliced
1 avocado, chopped
a handful of fresh coriander

If you go to any street market in Mexico they will be selling a variation on this soup. It is actually a cleansing broth with a hot-and-sour note, filled with chunky chicken and sweetcorn and topped with creamy avocado and swirls of crisp tortilla. The tortillas act like croutons and stay crisp on top but soak up all the lip-smacking juices underneath.

1. Heat 2 tablespoons of the oil in a large pan over a low heat. Add the onions and fry for 10 minutes, or until they have softened and started to turn a golden colour. For the last minute, add the garlic and chillies. Throw in the tomatoes, then pour over the stock. Add the sweetcorn and chicken breasts and simmer gently for 15 minutes.

2. Remove the chicken breast and set aside. Cook the soup for a further 10 minutes. Season to taste.

3. Shred the chicken and return it to the soup, along with any juices. Heat the remaining tablespoon of oil in a frying pan over a medium heat. Toss in the tortilla strips and fry for 3 minutes, or until crisp and golden. Ladle the soup into bowls and top with a sprinkling of tortillas, some avocado and coriander.

TIP: For an even speedier soup, why not add tortilla chips, unfried, instead of fried flour tortillas?

Gizzi Erskine's

CHICKEN SATAY NOODLE SOUP

INGREDIENTS

4 boneless chicken thighs
1 tsp ground coriander
½ tsp ground turmeric
½ tsp dried chillies
1 tsp sea salt
1 tbsp olive oil
1 × 400g (14oz) tin coconut milk
400ml (14fl oz) chicken stock
2½ tbsp yellow curry paste
1 tbsp peanut butter
2 tbsp Thai fish sauce (nam pla)
2 tbsp brown sugar
juice of ½ lemon
1 tbsp chilli oil
250g (9oz) rice noodles
sea salt and freshly ground black pepper

TO SERVE

a small bunch each fresh coriander and
   mint, chopped
¼ cucumber, sliced
2 spring onions, sliced
2 handfuls of beansprouts
1 red chilli, sliced
a large handful of roasted peanuts or
   cashews

I am an Asian food freak, and I make something Asian pretty much on a daily basis. It's so fast to cook and fresh.

1. Rub the chicken thighs with the ground coriander, turmeric, dried chillies and salt. Heat the oil in a frying pan over a lowish heat, add the thighs, skin-side down, and fry for 10 minutes, or until the skin is crispy. Turn them over and cook for a further 6 minutes. Set the pan aside and let the chicken rest, skin-side up, in the pan.

2. Put the coconut milk, stock, curry paste, peanut butter, fish sauce, brown sugar, lemon juice and chilli oil into a pan over a low heat and stir until the sugar has dissolved. Increase the heat, bring to the boil, and cook for 5 minutes. Season to taste.

3. Cook the rice noodles according to the packet instructions and divide among four bowls. Ladle the soup into the bowls, then top each serving with some fresh coriander, mint, cucumber, spring onions, beansprouts, chilli and chopped nuts. Slice the chicken thighs and distribute among the bowls. Serve piping hot.

Ken Hom's

VIETNAMESE BEEF AND SPINACH SOUP

INGREDIENTS

450g (1lb) fresh spinach
175g (6oz) lean fillet steak, cut into thin
　　slices about 5cm (2in) long
2 shallots, finely sliced
2 tbsp finely chopped garlic
3 tbsp Thai fish sauce (nam pla)
1.2 litres (2 pints) home-made chicken
　　stock (see page 10) or good-quality
　　bought stock
1 tbsp lemon juice
1 tsp sugar
1 small fresh red chilli, de-seeded and
　　chopped
freshly ground black pepper

This Vietnamese soup is similar to one I grew up with in our Chinese household. We used a variety of water spinach with a crisp stalk and distinctive flavour. I have found, however, that ordinary spinach works just as well. This light soup is typical of the subtle cuisine of Vietnam. It is easy to make, and much of the preparation can be done in advance.

1.　Remove the stalks from the spinach and wash the leaves well. Blanch the leaves for a few seconds in a large pan of boiling water until they are just wilted. Then drain well and refresh in cold water to prevent further cooking. Drain again, squeezing out excess water.

2.　Combine the slices of steak with the shallots, garlic, some freshly ground black pepper and 1 tablespoon of the fish sauce, then set aside. (The soup can be prepared in advance up to this point.)

3.　Just before you are ready to eat, bring the chicken stock to a simmer in a saucepan and season it with the remaining fish sauce, the lemon juice, sugar and chilli.

4.　Add the blanched spinach and stir in the beef and its marinade Bring the soup back to simmering point, add a few grindings of freshly ground black pepper to taste and serve at once.

Ainsley Harriott's

CHORIZO CHOWDER

INGREDIENTS

a knob of butter
1 small onion, finely chopped
4 garlic cloves, chopped
500g (1lb 2oz) floury potatoes such as
    Maris Piper or King Edward, cubed
1 leek, thinly sliced
1 tsp cayenne pepper
1 litre (1¾ pints) vegetable stock
250g (9oz) chorizo sausage, cut into 1cm
    (½in) wide slices, or 1cm (½in) dice
salt and freshly ground black pepper

TO SERVE
sprigs of fresh flat-leaf parsley
crusty bread (optional)

This warming soup makes a really satisfying winter supper or weekend lunch. Make sure you buy whole chorizo sausages and slice them yourself, as the slices in packets of pre-cut chorizo are too thin for this soup.

1. Heat the butter in a large pan and cook the onion, garlic and potatoes for 5 minutes until lightly golden. Add the leek and cayenne pepper and cook for a further 1 minute.

2. Add the stock and bring to the boil, then reduce the heat and simmer for 20 minutes until the potatoes are very soft and beginning to break up into the soup.

3. Using a potato masher, roughly mash the potatoes into the soup. Stir in the chorizo and simmer gently for 5 minutes until the orange-coloured oil from the chorizo rises to the surface of the soup. Season to taste, ladle into serving bowls and garnish with sprigs of flat-leaf parsley. Serve with lots of crusty bread for mopping up, if you like.

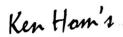

VIETNAMESE SOUP WITH BEANCURD

INGREDIENTS

100g (4oz) lean, boneless pork chops,
    cut into thin slices 5cm (2in) long
100g (4oz) raw prawns, shelled and
    de-veined, tails on
5 tsp Thai fish sauce (nam pla)
2 tbsp chopped spring onions (white part
    only)
450g (1lb) silken or firm beancurd
1.2 litres (2 pints) home-made chicken
    stock (see page 10) or good-quality
    bought stock
salt and freshly ground black pepper

TO GARNISH
3 tbsp chopped fresh chives
2 fresh red chillies, de-seeded and
    chopped

This hearty, colourful soup is light, yet is almost a meal in itself. I am reminded how similar it is to many of the soups from southern China. Easy to make, it relies on good chicken stock for its success.

1. In a bowl, combine the pork, prawns, 2 teaspoons of the fish sauce and the spring onions. Leave to marinate for about 10 minutes.

2. Gently cut the beancurd into 1cm (½in) cubes and leave to drain on kitchen paper for 10 minutes.

3. Pour the chicken stock into a saucepan and bring to a simmer. Add the marinated prawn and pork mixture and simmer for 2 minutes.

4. Add the beancurd and the remaining fish sauce and simmer for another 2 minutes. Season to taste with salt and pepper, then remove from the heat, garnish with the chives and chillies and serve.

Antonio Carluccio's

PEASANT SOUP

INGREDIENTS

2 tbsp olive oil
2 garlic cloves, finely chopped
1 carrot, peeled and diced
2 potatoes, peeled and diced
1 celery stick, diced
1 large tomato, peeled, de-seeded and
   diced
1.2 litres (2 pints) chicken stock
2 × 375g (13oz) tins cannellini or borlotti
   beans, drained
200g (7oz) *munnezzaglia* or spaghetti,
   broken into pieces
1 small chilli, finely chopped
2 fresh basil leaves, shredded
salt and freshly ground black pepper
1 tbsp virgin olive oil, to serve

This is my own version of a peasant soup which is also enjoyed in some of the best restaurants all over Italy. For this dish, the Neapolitans use pasta called *munnezzaglia* which is all the leftovers from different packets of pasta – for a quick meal, you can simply break spaghetti into smaller pieces. To speed up the preparation of this dish I suggest using tinned beans instead of dried.

1. Heat the oil and sweat the garlic. Add the vegetables and toss well. Pour in the stock, bring to the boil and simmer for 5 minutes. Add half the beans. Mash the remaining beans to a pulp with the back of a fork and add to the stock with the pasta, the chilli and the basil. Cook gently for another 8 minutes, stirring from time to time to prevent the mixture sticking. Season to taste and serve with a trickle of oil on top.

SAVOURY RICE SOUP

INGREDIENTS

100g (4oz) cooked long-grain white rice
1.2 litres (2 pints) home-made chicken
stock (see page 10) or good-quality
bought stock
3 tbsp Thai fish sauce (nam pla)
1½ tbsp vegetable oil
3 tbsp finely chopped garlic
freshly ground black pepper

TO GARNISH

2 spring onions, finely shredded
1 tbsp finely shredded fresh ginger
1–2 small fresh red or green Thai chillies,
de-seeded and finely shredded
a handful of fresh coriander

This is the Thai version of a gentle rice soup that can be found throughout Asia. The Chinese make it thick and creamy whereas *kao tom*, as it is known in Thailand, is more of a thin broth. However it is made, it is true comfort food, savoury and nurturing. Feel free to add your favourite cooked meat, poultry or seafood, or just serve it simply, with garnishes such as the ones listed below.

1. Combine the cooked rice and stock in a large saucepan and bring to a simmer. Add the fish sauce and some black pepper and simmer for 5 minutes.

2. Heat a wok or large frying pan over a medium heat. Add the oil and, when it is hot, stir in the garlic. Reduce the heat and stir-fry gently for 20 seconds, until the garlic is lightly browned. Remove and drain on kitchen paper.

3. Pour the rice and stock into the wok and simmer for 2 minutes. Turn into a soup tureen and serve at once with the garnishes, including the fried garlic.

Antonio Carluccio's

MINESTRONE

SERVES
4

INGREDIENTS

3 tbsp olive oil

1 onion, chopped

1 small garlic clove, chopped

2 rashers streaky bacon, rind removed and
finely chopped, or 25g (1oz) Parma ham,
finely chopped (optional)

4 celery sticks, diced

1 tomato, peeled, de-seeded and finely
chopped

1 large carrot, peeled and diced

2 potatoes, peeled and diced

a few fresh basil leaves, or 1 tbsp pesto
sauce

900ml (1½ pints) chicken stock

1 × 375g (13oz) tin borlotti beans, drained

100g (4oz) *tubettini* (fresh or dried)

75g (3oz) freshly grated Parmesan

salt and freshly ground black pepper

There are many different varieties of minestrone, each one
varying according to regional customs. I'll allow you to substitute
a stock cube for home-made stock in this recipe, but only if you
really have to!

1. Heat the oil and fry the onion and garlic with the chopped
   bacon or Parma ham (if using), until the onion is soft. Add the
   remaining vegetables, the basil or pesto, and toss well with
   the oil. Add the stock and bring to the boil. Cook for around
   10 minutes. Add salt and pepper to taste and stir in the borlotti
   beans and the pasta. Cook for about 10 minutes, or until the
   pasta is al dente. Serve hot, sprinkled with the grated Parmesan.

GINGERY CAULIFLOWER SOUP

INGREDIENTS

3 tbsp vegetable oil
175g (6oz) onions, chopped
2.5cm (1in) piece fresh ginger, cut into
    fine slivers
4 garlic cloves, chopped
1 tsp ground cumin
2 tsp ground coriander
¼ tsp ground turmeric
⅛–¼ tsp chilli powder
225g (8oz) potatoes, peeled and cut into
    rough 1cm (½in) dice
225g (8oz) cauliflower florets
1.2 litres (2 pints) chicken stock
150ml (5fl oz) single cream
salt, if needed

This soup may be served as an elegant first course at a grand dinner or as part of a simple lunch accompanied, perhaps, by a sandwich or salad or both. It may be made a day in advance and refrigerated. Reheat gently. It is a good idea to have the cumin, coriander, turmeric and chilli powder all measured into a small bowl before you start, as they go in together and cook very briefly.

1. Set the oil over highish heat in a good-sized saucepan. When hot, add the onions, ginger and garlic. Stir and fry for about 4 minutes or until the onions are somewhat browned. Put in the cumin, coriander, turmeric and chilli powder. Stir once and add the potatoes, cauliflower and chicken stock. If the stock is unsalted, add ¼ teaspoon salt. Stir and bring to the boil. Cover, turn the heat to low and simmer gently for 10 minutes or until the potatoes are tender.

2. Taste for salt, adding more if you like. Put the soup into a blender, in 2 batches or more as required, and blend thoroughly. Strain, pushing down to get all the pulp. Add the cream and mix. The soup may now be reheated and served.

Ainsley Harriott's

PEA, MINT AND SPINACH SOUP

INGREDIENTS

1 tbsp olive oil
25g (1oz) butter
1 onion, chopped
1 leek, chopped
1 fat garlic clove, crushed
225g (8oz) floury potatoes such as Maris
  Piper or King Edward, chopped
1.2 litres (2 pints) vegetable stock
250g (9oz) frozen garden peas, defrosted
75g (3oz) young leaf spinach
2 tbsp chopped fresh mint
salt and freshly ground black pepper
crème fraîche, to serve

This beautiful bright green soup is a taste of spring, but it can be enjoyed at any time of the year. Use frozen peas rather than fresh ones as they give a much better texture. This recipe creates very little washing-up – just blend the soup base until smooth, add the peas and spinach and blend again.

1. Heat the oil and butter in a large saucepan. Add the onion and leek and cook over a low heat for about 10 minutes, until tender but not coloured. Add the garlic and cook for a further 30 seconds.

2. Add the potatoes to the pan, pour in the stock and bring to the boil. Reduce the heat and simmer over a gentle heat for 15 minutes or until the potatoes are tender when tested with the point of a knife.

3. Pour the soup into a blender and whizz until smooth. Add the peas and spinach and blend again until the soup is bright green and almost smooth. Pour back into the pan, add the mint, then season and reheat gently. Pour the soup into warmed serving bowls, add a dollop of crème fraîche and a twist of pepper, and serve.

POSH TOMATO SOUP
WITH CAPPELLETTI

INGREDIENTS

3 red peppers, de-seeded and halved
5 vine tomatoes, halved
2 tbsp olive oil
1 onion, finely chopped
3 garlic cloves, finely chopped
100g (4oz) oak-smoked tomatoes, or 100g
   (4oz) sunblush tomatoes mixed with
   1 tsp smoked paprika
200ml (7fl oz) vegetable stock
3 fresh basil sprigs
100g (4oz) cappelletti of your choice
sea salt and freshly ground black pepper
pesto, to drizzle
grated Parmesan, to serve

Smoked tomatoes may not be widely available, but you should be able to find them at farmers' markets. If you can't, use the same quantity of sunblush tomatoes mixed with a teaspoon of smoked paprika. Cappelletti are simply tiny filled pasta (I love the ones filled with goats' cheese), similar to tortellini, but if you can't find them, use any small stuffed pasta you like.

1. Preheat the oven to 200°C/400°F/gas 6. Lay the pepper halves, cut-side up, on a baking sheet and top with the vine tomato halves. Drizzle with 1 tablespoon of olive oil and season with salt and pepper. Roast for 25 minutes, or until the peppers and tomatoes are starting to blacken and have softened.

2. Meanwhile, heat the remaining tablespoon of oil in a pan over a fairly low heat. Throw in the onions and fry for 10 minutes, so that they become really softened and start to caramelise and sweeten. For the last minute of the cooking time, add the garlic.

3. When the peppers and tomatoes are done, put them into a blender with the onions, garlic, smoked or sunblush tomatoes, vegetable stock and basil sprigs. Process for 2 minutes, until smooth, then return the soup to the pan. For a really smooth consistency, you can sieve it from the blender into the pan. Reheat very gently over a low heat.

4. Meanwhile, bring a pan of salted water to the boil. Add the cappelletti and boil for 1–2 minutes, then drain. Ladle the soup into bowls and top each serving with some of the cappelletti, a drizzle of pesto and a grating of Parmesan.

Ainsley Harriott's

RED LENTIL SOUP WITH LEMON YOGHURT

INGREDIENTS

1 tbsp olive oil
1 onion, finely chopped
2 carrots, finely diced
leaves from 1 sprig of fresh thyme
2 garlic cloves, finely chopped
1 red chilli, de-seeded and finely diced
1 tsp yellow mustard seeds
3 tomatoes, roughly diced
100g (4oz) dried red lentils
1.2 litres (2 pints) vegetable stock
4 tbsp Greek yoghurt
finely grated zest and juice of 1 small
    lemon
salt and freshly ground black pepper

This delicious and substantial vegetarian soup is a perfect warming dish for a cold winter's night. The red lentils are used to make a thick and tasty base to this soup. Alternatively, you could use yellow split peas, but these need soaking overnight before cooking.

1. Heat the oil in a large pan and cook the onion, carrots and thyme for about 3–4 minutes until beginning to soften. Add the garlic, chilli and mustard seeds and cook for a further couple of minutes.

2. Stir in the tomatoes, lentils and stock. Bring to the boil. Reduce the heat, cover and simmer gently for 30 minutes until the lentils are tender and easy to crush.

3. Mix together the yoghurt and half the lemon zest and season to taste. Drizzle the lemon juice into the soup and season with salt and pepper. Ladle the soup into warmed serving bowls, top with a spoonful of the lemon yoghurt and scatter over the remaining lemon zest and some freshly ground black pepper.

TIP: To prepare ahead you can make the soup up to the end of the lentil cooking time, then cool it thoroughly and freeze for up to a month. Defrost before reheating and completing the soup.

Gizzi Erskine's

VIETNAMESE PRAWNS AND LEMON GRASS

INGREDIENTS

1 tbsp groundnut oil
1 small onion, cut into slivers
2 spring onions, cut into 2.5cm (1in) pieces
12 large prawns, shelled and de-veined
juice of 4 lemons
4 tbsp Thai fish sauce (nam pla)
½ tsp chilli powder
2 tsp brown sugar
4 tbsp chicken stock
2 lime leaves, thinly sliced
2 shallots, finely chopped
1 stalk of lemon grass, finely chopped

TO SERVE
hot steamed rice
oriental greens

The minuscule amount of preparation needed for this dish is worth every second as it is so quick to cook. This is fast food at its best and most authentic. Fat, juicy prawns with a heady lemon grass sauce – truly too good to be believed, and made in less time and with less money than it would take to order it from a takeaway, to boot.

1. Heat the oil in a wok or frying pan until it is smoking, then add the onion, spring onions and prawns. Stir-fry for 2 minutes, or until the prawns start to curl up and get a bit of colour on them. Add all the remaining ingredients and bring to the boil for 1 minute. That's it! Serve with steamed rice and oriental greens.

SKATE WITH TOMATO, SAFFRON, GARLIC AND SULTANAS

INGREDIENTS

2 × 225g (8oz) skinned and trimmed skate wings

FOR THE SAUCE
100ml (3½fl oz) extra-virgin olive oil
6 garlic cloves, finely chopped
1 × 400g (14oz) tin good-quality plum tomatoes
30g (1¼oz) sultanas
pinch of saffron strands
pinch of crushed dried chillies
2 fresh bay leaves
1 tsp caster sugar
salt and freshly ground black pepper
1 tsp small capers, drained and rinsed, to serve

This dish is so easy to do, and it's something really quite special. In Cabra, Italy, they served it at room temperature as an antipasto along with some other dishes, but it's equally good served warm.

1. First make the sauce. Put the olive oil and garlic into a medium-sized pan. Place over a medium heat and, as soon as the garlic begins to sizzle, add the tomatoes, sultanas, saffron, dried chillies, bay leaves, sugar and ½ teaspoon salt. Bring up to a gentle simmer and leave to cook for 30 minutes, stirring every now and then and breaking up the tomatoes with a wooden spoon. Remove the bay leaves, season to taste with salt and pepper and keep warm.

2. Bring 1.5 litres (2½ pints) water to the boil in a large shallow pan. Add 1 tablespoon of salt and the skate wings and leave them to simmer gently for 10 minutes until cooked.

3. Lift the skate wings out of the water onto a board and cut each one into two or three pieces. Spoon slightly more than half the tomato sauce onto the base of a warmed oval serving dish and place the pieces of skate on top. Spoon the rest of the sauce down the centre of the skate, scatter with the capers and serve.

Raymond Blanc's

FILLETS OF HERRING WITH A POTATO SALAD

INGREDIENTS

8 × 50g (2oz) herring fillets

FOR THE MARINADE
200ml (7fl oz) water
85ml (3fl oz) white wine vinegar
½ garlic clove
1 tsp caster sugar
10 button onions, peeled and thinly sliced
    in small rings, blanched in boiling water
    for 10 seconds
1 fresh thyme sprig
½ bay leaf

FOR THE POTATO SALAD
400g (14oz) new potatoes (Pink Fir Apple
    or Jersey Royal), washed and not peeled
40g (1½oz) shallots, finely chopped
100ml (3½fl oz) dry white wine
50ml (2fl oz) white wine vinegar
50ml (2fl oz) groundnut oil
1 tsp chopped fresh flat-leaf parsley
sea salt and white pepper

If you use large fillets, ask your fishmonger to remove the bones for you. It is essential that the fish are fresh. Fresh sardines could easily replace the herrings.

1. Score the herring fillets on the skin side about 2mm (⅟₁₆in) deep, and place in a small container, flesh-side down. Mix together the marinade ingredients. Warm slightly in a small pan, then pour over the herring fillets. Seal with clingfilm and leave to marinate for 48 hours in the bottom of your fridge, turning occasionally.

2. To prepare the potato salad, cook the potatoes in simmering salted water for about 8–10 minutes according to size. Make sure they are not overcooked. Strain and leave to cool until warm. Cut into 5mm (¼in) slices with the skin on.

3. In a pan, mix the chopped shallots, wine and wine vinegar. Bring to the boil and boil for 30 seconds, then add the sliced, warm potatoes. Cover and cook for 1 minute over a low heat. Stir, then add the groundnut oil. Taste, season with sea salt and white pepper, then cool and add the parsley. To serve, place a small mound of potatoes in the middle of each plate and arrange the herring fillets on top. Spoon some of the marinating juices over with the onion rings.

Ken Hom's

FRESH VIETNAMESE SPRING ROLLS

INGREDIENTS

350g (12oz) raw prawns, shelled and
de-veined
50g (2oz) bean-thread (transparent)
noodles
225g (8oz) soft salad leaves
large bunches fresh basil, mint and
coriander
1 packet 20cm (8in) round rice paper
wrappers
225g (8oz) fresh beansprouts, rinsed

FOR THE PEANUT DIPPING SAUCE
2 tbsp Thai fish sauce (nam pla)
1–2 red chillies, de-seeded and chopped
1 tbsp finely chopped garlic
2 tbsp lime or lemon juice
5 tbsp water
1 tbsp sugar
3 tbsp roasted peanuts, crushed

I love these unusual, sparkling-fresh spring rolls. They make a perfect starter and I have often served them as a main course, especially on hot, humid summer evenings.

1. First make the peanut dipping sauce. Combine all the ingredients except the peanuts in a blender and process thoroughly. Pour into a small bowl and leave to stand for at least 10 minutes before using (the sauce can be prepared several hours in advance, if necessary).

2. Blanch the prawns in a pan of boiling salted water for 3 minutes, drain well and then cut them in half lengthways. Set aside until needed.

3. Soak the noodles in a large bowl of hot water for 15 minutes, until soft, then drain. Cut them into 7.5cm (3in) lengths, using scissors or a knife. Wash the salad leaves and spin them dry in a salad spinner. Do the same with the basil, mint and coriander.

4. When you are ready to make the spring rolls, fill a large bowl with warm water. Dip one of the rice paper rounds in the water and let it soften, then remove and drain on a tea towel. Put a large salad leaf on the softened rice paper wrapper. Add a spoonful of the noodles to the salad leaf, then add 3 basil leaves and 3 mint leaves. Then carefully roll the rice paper halfway up. Now place 3 pieces of prawn, 3 coriander sprigs and 2 tablespoons beansprouts on the wrapper. Fold the 2 ends in, then keep rolling until the entire rice paper is rolled up. Repeat with all the remaining ingredients. Cover the spring rolls with a damp tea-towel until you are ready to serve them (do not refrigerate; they are meant to be served at room temperature).

5. Just before serving, stir the crushed peanuts into the sauce. Cut each spring roll in half on the diagonal and serve with the sauce.

EASY CHICKEN KEBABS

SERVES
4

INGREDIENTS

4 boned, skinned chicken breast halves
   (about 550g/1¼lb)
¾ tsp salt
2 tbsp lemon juice
3 tbsp natural yoghurt
1 tbsp chickpea flour (also called gram
   flour or besan)
1 tsp very finely grated fresh ginger
2 garlic cloves, crushed to a pulp
¼ tsp chilli powder
¼ tsp ground turmeric
½ tsp ground cumin
½ tsp garam masala
4 tbsp melted butter or vegetable oil,
   for basting

You may serve these kebabs with drinks, as a first course or even as a light main dish. The pieces of meat may be skewered before grilling or they may just be spread out on a grilling tray.

1. Cut each breast half into halves, lengthways, and cut crossways into 2.5cm (1in) pieces. Put in a bowl. Rub with ½ teaspoon of the salt and the lemon juice.

2. Put the natural yoghurt into a separate small bowl. Add the chickpea flour and mix well. Now add the remaining salt, the ginger, garlic, chilli powder, turmeric, cumin and garam masala. Mix well and pour over the chicken pieces. Mix well again and set aside for 15 minutes or longer (you could even leave it overnight).

3. Preheat the grill. Thread the chicken pieces on to 4 skewers and balance the skewers on the raised edges of a grill rack. You could, as an alternative, spread the chicken pieces out on the grilling tray. Baste with the melted butter or oil. Grill the chicken pieces about 10cm (4in) from the source of heat for 5 minutes, basting once during this time. Turn the chicken pieces over, baste again and grill for 2–3 minutes or until just cooked through. Serve immediately.

Gizzi Erskine's

SMOKED HAM AND PICCALILLI SALAD

INGREDIENTS

½ cauliflower, broken into florets
30 green beans, trimmed
2 radishes, thinly sliced
2 carrots, thinly sliced
½ red onion, thinly sliced
2 gherkins, thinly sliced
1 head chicory
1 head Little Gem lettuce
200g (7oz) smoked ham, preferably torn
   from a ham hock, or thickly sliced ham,
   torn into pieces

FOR THE DRESSING

1 tsp English mustard powder
½ tsp ground turmeric
a pinch of allspice
a grating of nutmeg
½ garlic clove, grated
½ tsp sugar
2 tbsp cider vinegar
3 tbsp extra-virgin olive oil
sea salt

I love piccalilli and really wanted to find a way to put it into a salad, but, alas, it doesn't seem to work – it's all a bit too gungy. So instead I decided to make a salad with crunchy, peppery vegetables and drizzle it with a fantastic, fragrant, light, bright yellow dressing.

1. Bring a pan of salted water to the boil and throw in the cauliflower and beans. Boil for 2 minutes, then drain and plunge immediately into iced water to cool and stop the cooking process. When they have cooled, drain and place in a mixing bowl with the radishes, carrots, onion and gherkins.

2. To make the dressing, place all the ingredients in a clean jam jar, screw the lid on tightly and shake like crazy for 30 seconds. Pour half the dressing over the crunchy vegetables and mix thoroughly.

3. Separate, wash and dry the leaves of the chicory and Little Gem lettuce. Place on a large plate and drizzle with the rest of the dressing. Top with the crunchy vegetables and torn ham and serve immediately.

CABBAGE WITH SMOKED BACON AND CARAWAY SEEDS

SERVES
4

INGREDIENTS

1 Savoy cabbage
1 tbsp unsalted butter
150g (5oz) smoked streaky bacon, cut into fine strips
2 tsp caraway seeds, crushed
salt and freshly ground black pepper

Personally, I prefer to blanch the cabbage to remove some of its very powerful taste. It is always better to buy bacon that is in the piece rather than the already pre-cut slices; or get your butcher to slice the bacon in front of you. Newly sliced bacon will have a much better taste and texture.

1. To prepare the cabbage, cut off its stem and remove the coarse outer leaves. Halve the cabbage, cut out the cores and chop each half finely into 3mm (⅛in) thick slices. Wash in plenty of water, drain well and reserve.

2. Bring 2 litres (3½ pints) of water to a full boil with 30g (1¼oz) of salt, and boil the shredded cabbage for 5 minutes. Refresh in cold water, drain and reserve.

3. In a large cast-iron pan, melt the butter and sweat the bacon for 2 minutes. Add the cabbage and crushed caraway seeds, and mix well. Cover and cook for a further 5 minutes. Taste and adjust the seasoning, and serve.

Ken Hom's

CRISPY CORN CAKES

INGREDIENTS

450g (1lb) corn on the cob, or 275g (10oz) tinned sweetcorn
175g (6oz) minced fatty pork
2 tbsp finely chopped fresh coriander
2 tbsp finely chopped garlic
2 tbsp Thai fish sauce (nam pla)
½ tsp freshly ground white pepper
1 tsp sugar
1 tbsp cornflour
2 eggs, beaten
600ml (1 pint) vegetable oil, for deep-frying

TO GARNISH

a handful of fresh coriander sprigs
1 small cucumber, peeled and thinly sliced

These make a wonderfully enticing starter – a savoury mixture of corn and pork fried to crispy morsels. Serve them with sweet chilli dipping sauce. Their Thai name is *tod mun khao phod*.

1. If using corn on the cob, strip off the husks and the silk and cut off the kernels with a sharp knife or cleaver. You should end up with about 275g (10oz). If you are using tinned corn, drain it well.

2. Put half the corn in a blender, add all the remaining ingredients except the oil and blend to a purée. Pour this mixture into a bowl and stir in the rest of the corn.

3. Heat a wok or large frying pan over a high heat. Add the oil and, when it is very hot and slightly smoking, pour in a small ladleful of the corn mixture. Repeat until the wok is full. Reduce the heat to low and cook for 1–2 minutes, until the fritters are brown underneath, then turn them over and fry the other side.

4. Remove the fritters from the wok with a slotted spoon and drain on kitchen paper. Keep them warm while you cook the remaining fritters. Arrange on a warm platter, garnish with the coriander sprigs and sliced cucumber and serve at once.

Madhur Jaffrey's

SOUR POTATOES (KHATTE ALOO)

INGREDIENTS

7 medium-sized potatoes, boiled ahead of
time, and set aside for at least 2 hours
to cool

1½ tsp salt, or to taste

2–3 tbsp lemon juice, or to taste

2 tsp ground roasted cumin

¼ tsp freshly ground black pepper

¼–½ tsp cayenne pepper

2 tbsp finely chopped fresh coriander

This is an adaptation of a street-side snack to be found in
different forms all over North India.

1. Peel the cooled potatoes and dice them into 1cm (½in) cubes.
   Place in a large bowl. Add the remaining ingredients. Mix well.
   Check to see if salt and lemon juice are in correct proportions.
   To serve, place the potatoes on a platter accompanied by
   toothpicks. Serve with drinks.

Ainsley Harriot's
POMEGRANATE, ORANGE AND MINT SALAD

SERVES

4

INGREDIENTS

5–6 large oranges, plus 6 tbsp freshly
    squeezed orange juice
1 large pomegranate, seeds removed
    and any juices reserved (see tip)
2 tbsp olive oil
1 tbsp fresh mint leaves
salt and freshly ground black pepper

This salad makes a refreshing starter on a hot day, and is also good as a side salad or between courses as a palate cleanser. For a more substantial meal, feta cheese would be a great addition. So simple, yet delicious…

1. To get lovely slices of orange without any bitter pith, use a small sharp knife to take a slice off the top and bottom of the oranges so you can see the juicy flesh, then place on a chopping board. Carefully cut away the skin and pith, following the curve of the orange. Cut the fruit into horizontal slices, reserving any juice for the dressing.

2. Arrange the orange slices on a large glass serving dish and sprinkle over the pomegranate seeds.

3. To make the dressing, whisk together the olive oil, orange juice and any reserved pomegranate juice in a small bowl. Season to taste and drizzle over the salad. Scatter the mint leaves over the salad and serve.

TIP: Here's a quick tip for removing pomegranate seeds: cut the fruit in half, use a spoon to scrape out some of the seeds, then turn the fruit inside-out and scrape again.

Ken Ham's

CRISPY 'SEAWEED'

INGREDIENTS

1.25kg (2½lb) pak choy (Chinese white
    cabbage)
900ml (1½ pints) groundnut oil
1 tsp salt
2 tsp sugar
50g (2oz) pine nuts, lightly roasted, to
    garnish

This is one of the most popular Chinese restaurant dishes in the West. A special type of seaweed is used in China, but it is not readily available elsewhere, so Chinese cabbage is used instead. This is a good example of the adaptability of Chinese cuisine: if the original ingredients are not available, technique and ingenuity will overcome the deficiency. This dish is delicious and easy to make, and, speaking of adaptability, can also be tried with fresh spinach leaves.

1. Separate the stalks from the stem of the pak choy and then cut the green leaves from the white stalks. (Save the stalks; you can stir-fry them with garlic or use them for soup.)

2. Wash the leaves in several changes of cold water, then drain them thoroughly and dry in a salad spinner. Roll the leaves up tightly, a few at a time, and finely shred them into strips 5mm (¼in) wide.

3. Preheat the oven to 120°C/250°F/gas ½. Spread the cabbage strips out on a baking sheet and put in the preheated oven for 15 minutes to dry slightly. They should not be completely dry or they will burn when fried. Remove from the oven and leave to cool. This can be done the day before.

4. Heat a wok over a high heat, then add the oil. When the oil is hot and slightly smoking, deep-fry the cabbage strips in 3 or 4 batches. After about 30–40 seconds, when they turn crisp and green, remove them immediately from the wok and drain well on kitchen paper. Leave to cool.

5. Toss the crispy greens with the salt and sugar. Garnish with the pine nuts and serve.

LIGHT BITES
AND
LUNCHES

Gizzi Erskine's
CREAMY SMOKED SALMON AND PEA SPAGHETTI

INGREDIENTS

350g (12oz) dried spaghetti

150g (5oz) podded and shelled broad beans

150g (5oz) fresh or frozen garden peas

200ml (7fl oz) double cream

200ml (7fl oz) Greek yoghurt

2 large egg yolks

35g (1¼oz) freshly grated Parmesan

grated zest of 1 lemon

175g (6oz) smoked salmon (about 8 slices), cut into short ribbons

a small bunch fresh chives, snipped

sea salt and freshly ground black pepper

Spaghetti carbonara is a classic for a reason, but it is laden with cream and, therefore, also very guilt-inducing. So I decided to halve the cream content and replace the rest with Greek yoghurt. Having done this, it seemed natural to replace the smokiness of the bacon with smoked salmon. I then decided to add some green colour with the summery addition of broad beans and green peas, my favourite veggies, and finished with a hint of lemon to lift the dish.

1. Bring a large pan of salted water to the boil. Add the spaghetti and cook it according to the instructions on the packet. For the last 3 minutes of the cooking time add the broad beans and peas.

2. Meanwhile, mix together the cream, yoghurt, egg yolks, Parmesan, lemon zest and some salt and pepper to make a sauce. Drain the cooked pasta, beans and peas, leaving a few tablespoons of water in the bottom of the pan.

3. Return the pan to a low heat and pour in the sauce. Toss the pasta in the sauce, then add the smoked salmon and chives, mixing well until evenly incorporated and the salmon has cooked through. Serve piping hot.

TIP: If you like things quite lemony, add the zest of the whole lemon; otherwise, use just half.

Ken Hom's

FRAGRANT SINGAPORE-STYLE PRAWN CURRY

INGREDIENTS

1 lemon grass stalk

1 fresh red or green chilli

2 tbsp groundnut oil

100g (4oz) onion, coarsely chopped

2 tbsp finely chopped garlic

2 tsp finely chopped fresh ginger

450g (1lb) raw prawns, shelled and
    de-veined, tails on

2 tsp Madras curry paste

1 tsp chilli bean sauce

1 tsp sugar

2 tbsp water

1 tbsp Shaoxing rice wine or dry sherry

2 tsp light soy sauce

½ tsp salt

¼ tsp freshly ground black pepper

fresh coriander sprigs or lime wedges, to
    garnish

I enjoyed this delightful stir-fry dish for the first time in Singapore some years ago. Prawns have a delicate yet distinctive flavour, and the clean, mildly citrus touch of the lemon grass makes a perfect counterpart. The quick cooking style ensures that the two main ingredients remain at their best. Use fresh lemon grass whenever possible – in a dish like this it is worth a detour to obtain it. But if your search is in vain, you could substitute 2 tablespoons of grated lemon zest.

1. Peel off the tough outer layers of the lemon grass stalk, leaving the tender, whitish centre. Chop it finely. Cut the chilli in half and carefully remove and discard the seeds. Chop the chilli finely and combine it with the lemon grass.

2. Heat a wok or large frying pan over a high heat. Add the oil and, when it is very hot and slightly smoking, add the onion, garlic, ginger, lemon grass and chilli and stir-fry for 1 minute. Then add the prawns and stir-fry for another minute.

3. Now add all the remaining ingredients, except the coriander sprigs or lime wedges, and stir-fry for 4 minutes or until the prawns are firm and cooked. Turn the mixture onto a warm serving platter, garnish and serve at once.

Rick Stein's

CRAB WITH ROCKET, BASIL AND LEMON OLIVE OIL

INGREDIENTS

350g (12oz) fresh hand-picked white crabmeat

2 tsp fresh lemon juice

4 tsp extra-virgin olive oil, preferably lemon olive oil (see tip), plus extra for drizzling

8 fresh basil leaves, finely shredded

a handful of wild rocket leaves

sea salt and cracked black pepper

This is based on my memory of a dish from Assaggi, a modern Italian restaurant above a pub in London's Notting Hill. It is light, lively and perfectly composed for bringing the best out of fresh white crabmeat.

1. Put the crabmeat in a bowl and gently stir in the lemon juice, olive oil, basil and some seasoning to taste.

2. Make a small, tall pile of the crab mixture on four plates, placing them slightly off centre. Put a small pile of rocket leaves alongside. Drizzle a little more olive oil over the rocket and around the outside edge of the plates. Sprinkle the oil with a little sea salt and cracked black pepper and serve.

TIP: To make lemon olive oil, pare the zest from 1 lemon with a potato peeler. Cut the zest into thin strips and mix with 600ml (1 pint) of extra-virgin olive oil. Leave to infuse for 24 hours before using.

Raymond Blanc's

PAN-FRIED SALMON FILLET WITH SORREL SAUCE

INGREDIENTS

FOR THE SORREL SAUCE
1 shallot, finely chopped
50ml (2fl oz) dry white wine
100g (4oz) sorrel, stalks removed
100ml (3½fl oz) whipping cream
juice of ¼ lemon
1 plum tomato, de-seeded (but not
    skinned) and cut into 5mm (¼in) dice

FOR THE SALMON
4 × 175g (6oz) wild or organic salmon
    fillets, cut across from a medium-sized
    fish, skinned
20g (¾oz) unsalted butter
juice of ½ lemon
salt and white pepper

Sorrel used to grow wild in the fields of my native Franche-Comté and you can find it in the UK, too. It is very acidic and can be overwhelming, but combined with the mellow taste of salmon it works very well. Please try to buy the best salmon you can find. I am very well aware that wild or organic salmon costs a lot more than farmed salmon but it is definitely worth it.

1. To make the sorrel sauce, heat the shallot and white wine in a small pan on a high heat, bring to the boil and boil for 30 seconds, to evaporate the alcohol. Add the sorrel, whipping cream, lemon juice, 2 pinches of salt and 2 pinches of white pepper. Bring to the boil and cook, stirring, for 1 minute, until the cream has thickened a little. Do not be alarmed if the sorrel starts changing colour from bright green to a brownish green. This is completely normal. Add the diced tomato and set aside.

2. Season the salmon fillets with 2 pinches of salt and 2 pinches of white pepper. On a medium heat, in a large frying pan, melt the butter until it is foaming. Add the salmon fillets and fry for 2–3 minutes on each side, depending on the thickness of the fillet. Remove from the heat and squeeze a little lemon juice over each fillet. Reheat the sorrel sauce and divide it among four serving plates. Arrange the salmon on the plates and serve immediately.

Rick Stein's

THE PADSTOW DELI CRAB SANDWICH WITH PARSLEY, CHILLI, LEMON AND ROCKET

MAKES
6

INGREDIENTS

12 thin slices of wholemeal bread
75g (3oz) butter, softened
5 tbsp mayonnaise (see tip)
1 tsp fresh lemon juice
½–1 red chilli, depending on heat,
 de-seeded and finely chopped
500g (1lb 2oz) fresh hand-picked white
 crabmeat
2 tbsp chopped fresh flat-leaf parsley
50g (2oz) rocket
salt

If crab came out of its shell in lovely firm pieces like lobster, I wouldn't be surprised if it fetched more money, because I often think it's got a better flavour than lobster. Fortunately, crab is not enormously expensive and it's really good in sandwiches. This is a great favourite at our deli.

1. Butter the slices of bread and put them to one side.

2. Put the mayonnaise into a small bowl and stir in the lemon juice and chilli. Put the crabmeat and parsley into another bowl and lightly stir through the mayonnaise mixture. Season to taste with a little salt.

3. Put six slices of the bread, buttered sides up, on a board and spoon over the crab mixture. Cover with a generous layer of the rocket leaves and then top with the remaining slices of bread. Cut each sandwich diagonally into halves or quarters and serve immediately.

TIP: To make 300ml (10fl oz) mayonnaise, put 2 egg yolks into a mixing bowl with 2 teaspoons of white wine vinegar and ½ teaspoon of salt. Rest the bowl on a cloth to stop it slipping, then lightly whisk to break the egg yolks. Use a wire whisk to beat in 300ml (10fl oz) olive or sunflower oil, adding the oil a few drops at a time until you have incorporated it all. Alternatively, put a whole egg, the vinegar and salt into a food processor. Turn on the machine and slowly add the oil until you have a thick emulsion.

Madhur Jaffrey's

CURRIED TUNA (TUNA KI KARI)

INGREDIENTS

1½ tbsp vegetable oil

50g (2oz) onion, cut into very fine half-rings

1 garlic clove, very finely chopped

1 tsp curry powder

1 × 175g (6oz) tin good-quality tuna, packed in oil

½–1 fresh, hot green chilli, cut into very fine rounds

1cm (½in) piece fresh ginger, cut into very fine slices, then into very fine strips

2–3 tbsp chopped fresh coriander

salt and freshly ground black pepper

This recipe, which is as good as it is simple, comes from Chun Kern, my friend from the Himalayan hills who now lives in the United States. You may eat this in sandwiches, on toast, take it on picnics (I always do) or use it as a stuffing for 'turnover'-type patties made with store-bought puff pastry. It is excellent eaten plain with a variety of salads. Use a good-quality tinned tuna packed in oil. I do not drain it as the oil prevents the tuna from drying out. Also, a good curry powder provides a useful short cut.

1. Put the oil in a non-stick frying pan and set over medium-high heat. When hot, add the onion and garlic. Stir and fry until the onion turns brown at the edges. Put in the curry powder, stir once or twice. Add the tuna. Stir it around and break up any big lumps. Turn the heat to low. Add the green chilli, ginger and coriander. Stir to mix. Check for salt, adding it if needed. Add a generous amount of black pepper. Mix well and turn off the heat. Serve hot, at room temperature or cold.

Ken Hom's

TEN-MINUTE SALMON WITH
SPRING ONION SAUCE

INGREDIENTS

450g (1lb) fresh salmon fillets
2 tsp salt
½ tsp freshly ground white or black
pepper

FOR THE SAUCE

6 tbsp coarsely chopped spring onions
1 tbsp finely chopped fresh ginger
(see tip)
1½ tbsp groundnut oil
2 tsp sesame oil

We Chinese prefer no more than a few hours to elapse between the catching and cooking of fish. Indeed, in many markets in southern China and Hong Kong, fish are sold live. You can select the fish of your choice while it swims around in special glass tanks and then take it home or to a restaurant to be cooked. Serve this truly quick and elegant dish as part of a main course, accompanied by an easy vegetable dish and rice, or as a starter. Sea bass or plaice fillets can be substituted.

1. Rub the salmon fillets with half the salt and the pepper. Bring 600ml (1 pint) of water to a simmer in a frying pan. Add the salmon, simmer for 2–3 minutes, cover tightly and turn off the heat. Let stand for 8 minutes.

2. To make the sauce, combine the spring onions, ginger and remaining salt in a small bowl. In a small pan, combine the oils and heat to smoking point.

3. Remove the salmon from the water and place on a plate. Scatter over the spring onion mixture, then pour over the hot oils and serve.

TIP: Peeled fresh ginger can be stored in a glass jar, covered in rice wine or sherry, and sealed. It will keep for several months, and has the added benefit of producing a flavoured wine that can be used in cooking.

Rick Stein's

JACK'S MUD CRAB OMELETTE

INGREDIENTS

FOR THE NAM PRIK SAUCE

juice of 1 lime
1 large garlic clove
1 tbsp Thai sweet chilli and dried shrimp
  sauce
½ tsp Indonesian red chilli paste
25ml (1fl oz) ketjap manis (sweet soy
  sauce)
100g (4oz) light muscovado sugar
2 tbsp chopped fresh coriander
1 tsp chopped fresh mint

FOR THE VEGETABLE STIR-FRY

1 tbsp sunflower oil
40g (1½oz) beansprouts
40g (1½oz) mangetout, thinly shredded
½ red pepper, de-seeded and cut into
  strips
½ medium carrot, cut into strips
½ red onion, sliced
4 fresh shiitake mushrooms, thinly sliced
4 oyster mushrooms, torn into fine strips
15g (½oz) Japanese pickled ginger,
  shredded
salt and freshly ground black pepper

FOR THE OMELETTES

4 tbsp sunflower oil
12 large eggs, beaten
225g (8oz) fresh white crabmeat

Jack was a customer at Two Small Rooms, a delightful restaurant in Brisbane, Australia, that I used to visit too. He visited the restaurant every Saturday night and ordered this omelette every time, followed by a steak.

1. To make the sauce, put the lime juice and garlic into a liquidiser and whizz until smooth. Add all the remaining sauce ingredients and blend well. Add enough water to make a smooth, sauce-like consistency, then pass through a fine sieve.

2. For the vegetable stir-fry, heat the oil in a frying pan or wok, add all the vegetables and stir-fry for 1–2 minutes until just cooked but still crunchy. Add the pickled ginger and toss for a few seconds to heat through.

3. Drizzle some of the nam prik sauce over each serving plate in a zigzag pattern and then put the stir-fried vegetables in the centre of each plate.

4. For the omelettes, heat a 20–23cm (8–9in) omelette pan over a medium heat, add 1 tablespoon of the oil and, when it is hot, a quarter of the beaten eggs. Move the mixture over the base of the pan with the back of a fork until it begins to set, then stop stirring and cook until it is just a little moist on top – about 2 minutes in total. Put a quarter of the crab meat down the centre of the omelette and season to taste with salt and pepper. Fold the sides of the omelette over the crab meat and place on the stir-fried vegetables. Serve immediately and cook the remaining omelettes in the same way.

Madhur Jaffrey's

SILKEN CHICKEN TIKKA KEBABS (RESHMI TIKKA KEBAB)

INGREDIENTS

675g (1½lb) boned and skinned chicken
  breasts, cut into 2.5cm (1in) pieces
1¼ tsp salt
3 tbsp lemon juice
1 tbsp very finely grated fresh ginger
2 garlic cloves, crushed to a pulp
1 tsp ground cumin
1 tsp bright red paprika
½–¾ tsp cayenne pepper
6 tbsp whipping cream
½ tsp garam masala
3 tbsp corn oil or peanut oil, for brushing

These kebabs are very easy to prepare and have a delicate, delicious flavour. This dish could serve eight people as a starter.

1. Put the chicken in a bowl. Add the salt and lemon juice and rub them in. Prod the chicken pieces lightly with the tip of a knife and rub the seasonings in again. Set aside for 20 minutes. Then add the ginger, garlic, cumin, paprika, cayenne pepper, cream and garam masala. Mix well, cover and refrigerate for 6–8 hours. (Longer will not hurt.)

2. Just before serving, preheat the grill. Thread the chicken pieces onto 2–4 skewers (the flat, sword-like ones are best). Brush with oil and balance the skewers on the rim of a shallow baking tray. Place about 13cm (5in) from the source of heat and grill for about 6 minutes on each side or until lightly browned and cooked through.

Ainsley Harriot's

AMERICAN-STYLE SEARED CHICKEN SALAD

INGREDIENTS

3 tbsp mayonnaise
1 tbsp crème fraîche
2 garlic cloves,crushed
1 tsp Dijon mustard
1 tspWorcestershire sauce
¼ tsp Tabasco sauce
2 anchovy fillets, crushed to a paste
4 tbsp olive oil
1 tsp sweet paprika
2 tbsp chopped fresh flat-leaf parsley
2 chicken breast fillets
2 slices country-style bread, crusts
   removed and cut into cubes
1 large cos lettuce
40g (1½oz) freshly grated Parmesan
salt and freshly ground black pepper

This is a variation on the famous Caesar salad but is much easier to prepare. If time allows, rub the paprika mixture into the chicken, cover with clingfilm and chill overnight to allow the flavours to penetrate the flesh.

1. Place the mayonnaise in a small bowl and mix in the crème fraîche. Add half the garlic and the mustard, Worcestershire sauce, Tabasco sauce and anchovies, then beat until well combined. Season to taste. Cover with clingfilm and chill until ready to use.

2. Heat a griddle pan until searing hot. Place half the olive oil in a shallow, non-metallic dish and mix with the remaining garlic plus the paprika, parsley and a teaspoon each of salt and pepper. Slash the chicken fillets and rub the oil mixture into the flesh, then place in the griddle pan and cook for 10–12 minutes, turning once, until cooked through and completely tender. Transfer to a plate and leave to rest for a minute or two.

3. Meanwhile, make some croûtons. Heat a frying pan. Toss the bread cubes in a bowl with the remaining oil and season generously. Add to the heated pan and sauté. For 6–8 minutes until evenly golden.

4. Break the large outer lettuce leaves roughly, keeping the smaller leaves whole. Toss with the mayonnaise mixture and two-thirds of the grated Parmesan. Arrange the leaves in the centre of 2 plates, scatter with the croûtons, then garnish with the remaining Parmesan. Carve each chicken breast on the diagonal and arrange on the salads to serve.

YAKITORI CHICKEN SKEWERS

INGREDIENTS

6 tbsp Japanese soy sauce, plus extra for
dipping
3 tbsp mirin
2 tbsp sake
1 tbsp caster sugar
450g (1lb) boneless, skinless chicken
thighs

These skewers are incredibly easy to make but taste so delicious they'll be gone before you know it. Traditional Japanese ingredients are now becoming much more widely available so look out for them in your local supermarket.

1. Put the soy sauce, mirin, sake and sugar into a small pan. Bring to the boil, then reduce the heat and simmer for about 5 minutes, stirring occasionally, until the mixture has reduced and become slightly syrupy. Place in a shallow non-metallic dish and leave to cool.

2. Cut the chicken thighs into 2cm (¾in) pieces and add to the cooled marinade. Cover with clingfilm and chill for at least 2 hours, or overnight if time allows.

3. Light the barbecue. Soak 8 × 15cm (6in) wooden skewers in a shallow dish of cold water for 30 minutes to prevent them from burning on the barbecue.

4. Thread the chicken onto skewers and barbecue for 6–8 minutes on medium hot coals, turning and basting with the marinade now and then. Arrange onto warmed plates to serve, with small bowls of soy sauce on the side for dipping.

Ken Hom's

THAI BARBECUE CHICKEN

INGREDIENTS

900g (2lb) chicken thighs, with bone in
a handful of fresh coriander sprigs, to
    garnish

FOR THE MARINADE
2 tbsp Thai fish sauce (nam pla)
3 tbsp coarsely chopped garlic
3 tbsp chopped fresh coriander
2 small, fresh Thai red or green chillies,
    de-seeded and chopped
4 kaffir lime leaves or 1 tbsp lime zest
2 tsp sugar
1 tbsp Shaoxing rice wine or dry sherry
1 tsp ground turmeric
2 tsp Thai red curry paste
1 tsp salt
½ tsp freshly ground black pepper
4 tbsp tinned coconut milk

The streets of Thailand are redolent with the aromas of smoky grilled foods. One of the most popular dishes is *gai yang*, a tasty version of barbecue chicken. It is made using chicken thighs, which are not only meatier than breasts, but tend to stay moist despite the intense heat of the grill. The secret is to marinate the chicken overnight if you have the time to do so. Once that is done, the rest is quite easy. It makes a memorable picnic dish or summer meal, served at room temperature.

1. Put all the marinade ingredients in a blender and process to a smooth purée.

2. Blot the chicken thighs dry on kitchen paper. Put them in a large bowl, add the marinade and mix well. Cover with clingfilm and leave to marinate in the fridge overnight. The next day, remove the chicken from the fridge and leave at room temperature for 40 minutes before cooking.

3. Light a barbecue or preheat the grill to high. When the charcoal is ash white or the grill is very hot, grill the thighs for 10 minutes on each side or until cooked through. Place on a warm platter, garnish with the coriander sprigs and serve immediately, or allow to cool and serve at room temperature.

Gizzi Erskine's

THE ULTIMATE STEAK
AND STILTON SANDWICH

INGREDIENTS

FOR THE CARAMELISED ONIONS
2 tbsp olive oil, plus extra for drizzling
1 large red onion, finely sliced

FOR THE STEAK SANDWICHES
2 sirloins or rump steaks, about 200g (7oz)
 each
4 mini ciabatta or crusty rolls
100g (4oz) Stilton cheese
100g (4oz) watercress
2 tsp English mustard
sea salt and freshly ground black pepper

A good steak sandwich is not to be missed, but with the inclusion of Stilton its deliciousness becomes stratospheric! It's worth spending the time to make the caramelised onions, but no one is going to frown at you if you cheat with some onion marmalade instead.

1. Heat the olive oil in a frying pan, add the onion and season. Cook on a medium heat for 10–15 minutes until golden and caramelised. Remove from the heat and set aside.

2. Heat a griddle pan until smoking. Season the steaks well with salt and pepper then griddle (chargrill) for 2–3 minutes each side for rare or medium. Transfer the steaks to a plate and leave to rest for 10 minutes.

3. Slice the rolls in half horizontally. Place them on the griddle cut-face down for a minute until a little charred. Whip them off the griddle, then drizzle with a little olive oil. Cut the steaks into slices about 1cm (½in) thick. To serve, fill each roll with steak slices, Stilton, watercress, caramelised onions and some mustard.

Ken Hom's

FRAGRANT THAI MEATBALLS

INGREDIENTS

100g (4oz) minced beef
100g (4oz) minced fatty pork
1 egg white
2 tbsp very cold water
1 tsp salt
½ tsp freshly ground black pepper
2 tbsp finely chopped garlic
3 tbsp finely chopped fresh coriander
2 tbsp finely chopped spring onions
1 tbsp Thai fish sauce (nam pla)
2 tsp sugar
plain flour, for dusting
450ml (15fl oz) vegetable oil, for
  deep-frying

Walking through Bangkok, one is always pleasantly aware of exotic, mouth-watering aromas emanating from the many small restaurants and street stalls that line the thoroughfares. These meatballs are typical Thai street food. What makes them so deliciously savoury is the spices blending into the succulent beef and pork, while the egg white gives them a delicate, light texture. They are very easy to prepare and make.

1. Process the beef and pork in a food processor for a few seconds. Slowly add the egg white and cold water and process for a few more seconds, until fully incorporated into the meat. Add all the remaining ingredients except the flour and vegetable oil and process for about a minute, until the mixture becomes a light paste.

2. Using your hands, shape the mixture into about 10 × 4cm (1½in) balls. Dust them evenly with flour, shaking off any excess. The meatballs will be quite fragile and soft.

3. Heat a wok or large frying pan over a high heat. Add the oil and, when it is very hot and slightly smoking, gently drop in as many meatballs as will fit easily in one layer. Fry for about 4 minutes, adjusting the heat as necessary, until they are crisp and browned all over and cooked through. Remove with a slotted spoon and drain on kitchen paper, then repeat the process with any remaining meatballs. Serve at once.

Antonio Carluccio's

PENNE RIGATE WITH SAUSAGE

SERVES
4

INGREDIENTS

75g (3oz) butter
1 small onion, chopped
1 garlic clove, finely chopped
300g (11oz) pork sausage meat or
　sausages (*luganega* type)
1 sprig fresh rosemary, finely chopped
150ml (5fl oz) dry white wine
pinch of freshly grated nutmeg
pinch of ground cloves
375g (13oz) dried penne rigate or penne
75g (3oz) freshly grated Parmesan
salt and freshly ground black pepper

The ribbed penne rigate are very popular in Italy, and abroad too. Usually, an Italian trattoria offers them *all'arrabbiata* – with chilli or with a tuna-fish sauce. (They are also used in timbales.) This version is based on the best-quality pork sausage meat you can find (100 per cent pork, if possible) and it is very delicious.

1.　Heat the butter and gently fry the onion and the garlic. Break up the sausage meat with a fork (if using sausages, remove the skin before breaking up the meat). Add to the pan and gently fry until well browned. Add the rosemary and the wine, and cook slowly for 10 minutes. Add the nutmeg, cloves and a little salt and pepper.

2.　Meanwhile, cook the pasta for 7–8 minutes or until al dente, and drain. Mix with the sausage mixture and the Parmesan.

Gizzi Erskine's
FILIPINO FRIED RICE WITH FRIED EGGS AND CHORIZO

SERVES
4

INGREDIENTS

2 tbsp groundnut oil

2–3 garlic cloves, chopped

450g (1lb) cooked long-grain rice

1–2 tbsp Filipino or Thai fish sauce (nam pla)

sea salt and freshly ground black pepper

TO SERVE

2 tbsp groundnut oil

3 whole fresh chorizo sausages, sliced diagonally

4 eggs

4–6 tbsp coconut vinegar, or rice wine vinegar, for dipping (optional)

Having never been to the Philippines I can't vouch for whether it's authentic, but it's a damn great dish. Plus, what a great way of using up leftover rice, and it's delicious served on its own or with meat and poultry dishes. If you don't have any leftover rice, cook 225g (8oz) the day before, using the absorption method, and keep it in the fridge.

1. Add the 2 tablespoons of oil to a wok or a heavy pan over a medium heat. Add the garlic, stirring it often, and fry until fragrant and golden. Toss in the rice, breaking up any lumps, then stir in the fish sauce. Season with salt, if needed, and black pepper, then turn off the heat and cover with a lid to keep warm.

2. Just before serving, place 1 tablespoon of the oil in a heavy pan over a medium heat. Add the chorizo and fry until crispy on both sides. Remove from the pan and drain on kitchen paper. Meanwhile, in a separate pan, heat 1 tablespoon of oil over a low to medium heat and fry the eggs, making sure the yolk remains soft and runny.

3. Tip the rice on to individual plates, place an egg on top, and arrange the fried chorizo around the edge. Serve warm with coconut or rice wine vinegar, if you like.

PETITS POIS À LA FRANÇAISE

SERVES
4

INGREDIENTS

25g (1oz) unsalted butter
20 baby onions
50g (2oz) smoked streaky bacon, rind removed, cut into lardons (little strips) 3mm (⅛ in) thick
200ml (7fl oz) water
3 pinches of sugar
400g (14oz) shelled young fresh peas or frozen peas
1 Webbs lettuce or other soft lettuce, leaves separated
salt and freshly ground black pepper

Freshly picked young peas are always the best but frozen peas are excellent, too. If you prefer, you could omit the bacon and stir in some parsley and chervil at the end instead to create a delicious vegetarian alternative.

1. On a low heat, in a small pan, melt the butter, add the baby onions and bacon lardons, and soften for 2–3 minutes, without colouring.

2. Add the water, sugar, 5 pinches of salt and a pinch of black pepper, and bring to the boil. Cover and reduce the heat to just below a simmer (with bubbles just breaking the surface). Cook for 15–20 minutes, until the onions are translucent, soft and melting but still retain some texture.

3. Remove the lid, turn the heat to high and add the peas and lettuce leaves. Stir, then cover and cook for 1–2 minutes, until the peas are tender. Taste and adjust the seasoning if required.

Madhur Jaffrey's

SCRAMBLED EGGS, INDIAN STYLE

SERVES
2–3

INGREDIENTS

3 tbsp butter
½ medium onion, finely chopped
1 small tomato, chopped
1 tbsp chopped fresh coriander
½–1 hot green chilli, finely sliced
4 medium or large eggs, well beaten
salt and pepper

While some Indians eat their scrambled eggs with toast, others eat them with hot parathas, chapatis or pooris.

1. Melt the butter in a 25cm (10in) frying pan over medium heat. Add the onion and sauté for a minute or until it begins to turn translucent. Add the chopped tomato, coriander and sliced green chilli. Stir and cook for 3–4 minutes or until the tomatoes soften a bit.

2. Pour in the beaten eggs. Sprinkle on salt and pepper lightly. Stir and move the eggs around with a fork. Indians like their scrambled eggs rather hard (cooked about 3 minutes), but you can stop whenever the desired consistency has been achieved.

LIGHT BITES AND LUNCHES

Ainsley Harriott's
COURGETTE, CORIANDER AND PARMESAN RÖSTIS

SERVES
4

INGREDIENTS

550g (1¼lb) courgettes, coarsely grated
100g (4oz) ground rice
3 tbsp shredded fresh coriander
75g (3oz) Parmesan, freshly grated
1 egg, lightly beaten
1 tsp finely grated lemon zest, plus 1 tbsp
   lemon juice
50g (2oz) flaked almonds
120ml (4fl oz) olive oil
1 ripe tomato, de-seeded and finely diced
1 shallot, finely chopped
salt and freshly ground black pepper

TO SERVE
100g (4oz) wild rocket or watercress
lemon wedges

Courgettes are such a versatile vegetable: here I've combined them with the freshness of lemon and the fragrance of coriander and accompanied them with a salad, and I'm sure these fritters will turn into a firm favourite.

1. Preheat the oven to 100°C/200°F/gas ⅓. Squeeze the courgettes dry in a clean tea towel and tip into a large bowl. Mix in the ground rice, coriander, Parmesan, egg, lemon zest and almonds. Season to taste and divide into 16 evenly sized balls, then flatten slightly into patties.

2. Heat 2 tablespoons of the olive oil in a large, non-stick frying pan. Carefully add half the patties. Cook for 2–3 minutes on each side or until cooked through, crisp and golden. Drain on kitchen paper and keep warm in the oven. Repeat with a further 2 tablespoons of oil and the remaining patties.

3. To make the dressing, place the remaining oil in a bowl and add the tomato, shallot and lemon juice, and season to taste. Whisk until well combined. Divide the salad leaves among serving plates and drizzle over the dressing. Add the fritters and garnish with the lemon wedges to serve.

TIP: Courgettes have a naturally high water content – squeezing them dry before they are fried ensures that the fritters are lovely and crisp when cooked.

Antonio Carluccio's

SPAGHETTINI WITH TOMATO AND BASIL

INGREDIENTS

50g (2oz) butter
1 small onion, finely chopped, or 4 spring
    onions, finely chopped
3 large, ripe tomatoes, peeled, de-seeded
    and roughly chopped
8 fresh basil leaves, shredded
400g (14oz) spaghettini (fresh or dried)
50g (2oz) freshly grated Parmesan
salt

This is one of the simplest sauces. If you use garlic instead of onion, and olive oil instead of butter, you obtain a Neapolitan sauce that is equally good. If you manage to find the best ripe tomatoes, you can leave out the cheese because the taste will be rich and fine without it.

1. Heat the butter and gently fry the onion or spring onions until beginning to brown. Add the tomatoes and fry for another 3–4 minutes. Add the basil and salt to taste.

2. Meanwhile, cook the pasta according to the packet instructions or until al dente. Mix with the sauce and serve sprinkled with the grated Parmesan.

Madhur Jaffrey's

AUBERGINE COOKED WITH CRUSHED MUSTARD SEEDS AND YOGHURT

INGREDIENTS

450–675g (1–1½lb) aubergine
1½ tbsp whole black mustard seeds
⅛ tsp cayenne pepper
7 tbsp mustard oil or vegetable oil
1 tbsp panchphoran (see tip)
1½ tsp salt
250ml (8fl oz) natural yoghurt
⅛ tsp freshly ground black pepper
¼ tsp freshly ground cardamom seeds

This quick-cooking dish from eastern India uses three ingredients that are very typical of Bengali cooking – mustard oil, panchphoran and crushed black mustard seeds.

1. Discard the stem end of the aubergine and dice the aubergine into 2.5cm (1in) cubes.

2. Grind the mustard seeds lightly in a coffee grinder and then empty into a bowl. Add the cayenne and 250ml (8fl oz) water. Mix and set aside.

3. Heat the oil in a 30cm (12in) frying or sauté pan over a medium-high heat. When hot, put in the panchphoran. Stir the spices once. Immediately add the mustard seed mixture, the cubed aubergine and 1 teaspoon salt. Keep stirring and cooking until most of the liquid is absorbed. Add another 250ml (8fl oz) of water, cover, and turn the heat to low. Simmer gently for about 15 minutes or until the aubergine pieces are quite tender. Remove the cover and turn up the heat to boil off about half the liquid.

4. Just before serving, beat the yoghurt and ½ teaspoon salt with a fork until it becomes a smooth paste and pour over the aubergine. Heat through, but do not bring to the boil. Sprinkle black pepper and ground cardamom over the aubergine, stir and serve at once.

TIP: Panchphoran is a Bengali spice mixture consisting of fennel seeds, mustard seeds, fenugreek seeds, cumin seeds and kalongi (nigella seeds) mixed in equal proportion.

Gizzi Erskine's
FRIED GNOCCHI WITH TOMATO AND GOATS' CHEESE SAUCE

INGREDIENTS

30g (1¼oz) butter
450g (1lb) fresh shop-bought gnocchi, cooked for 2 minutes in salted, boiling water
freshly grated Parmesan, to serve

FOR THE SAUCE

1 tbsp olive oil
1 onion, finely chopped
3 garlic cloves, finely chopped
1 × 400g (14oz) tin chopped tomatoes
1 tbsp sun-dried tomato paste or tomato purée
a splash of good-quality sherry vinegar
a few splashes of Tabasco
1 tsp sugar
a small bunch fresh basil leaves, torn
100g (4oz) fresh soft goats' cheese
sea salt and freshly ground black pepper

As scrummy as gnocchi are in their own right, frying them gently in butter lifts them to a whole new level. The middles are like fluffy clouds of potato and the outsides become crispy and golden like a potato croquette.

1. First make the sauce. Heat the oil in a saucepan. Add the onion and fry gently for 8 minutes or until it has softened and begun to turn golden.

2. Add the garlic and fry for a further minute. Tip in the chopped tomatoes, tomato paste or purée, sherry vinegar, Tabasco, sugar, half the basil and some salt and pepper, and leave to bubble away gently on a low heat for 20 minutes. The sauce will have thickened up nicely by this stage. Crumble in the goats' cheese and stir gently as if to tease it into melting.

3. Melt the butter in a frying pan and, working in batches, add the precooked gnocchi. Fry for 2 minutes on each side, or until they have crisped up and are golden. Drain the finished gnocchi on kitchen paper while you cook the rest. Serve with a dollop of sauce, the remaining torn basil and a grating of Parmesan.

Antonio Carluccio's

TROFIE WITH PESTO

INGREDIENTS

4 garlic cloves
40–50 fresh basil leaves
10g (¼oz) coarse sea salt
50g (2oz) pine kernels
extra-virgin olive oil, as required
50g (2oz) freshly grated Parmesan
500g (1lb 2oz) dried trofie, *strozzapreti*
  or fusilli

Trofie is a particular pasta shape from Liguria. It is usually home-made but you can find it in good Italian shops. Alternatively, you can use *strozzapreti* or fusilli instead.

1. Put the garlic and basil leaves in a mortar and add the salt, which under the pestle and the power of your elbow will function as a grinder. Also add the pine kernels and reduce to a paste, slowly drizzling in some oil. Incorporate the Parmesan and continue to grind with the pestle, adding enough oil to achieve a very smooth and homogenous sauce of a brilliant green colour.

2. Boil the pasta in slightly salted water according to the packet instructions. Drain, transfer to a warmed china bowl and mix thoroughly with the pesto sauce. Serve immediately. The sauce should cover each piece of pasta and there should be none left on the plate!

Madhur Jaffrey's
EGGS WITH FRESH GREEN HERBS
(HARE MASALE KA OMLATE)

INGREDIENTS

5 large eggs

2 tbsp vegetable oil

3 spring onions, cut into fine rounds (the white as well as the green sections)

¼ tsp very finely chopped garlic

3 tbsp finely chopped fresh coriander

1–2 fresh, hot green chillies, sliced into fine rounds

½ tsp very finely chopped fresh ginger

generous pinch of ground turmeric

1½ tsp lemon juice

⅓ tsp sugar

salt and freshly ground black pepper

This may be served at breakfasts and brunches as soon as it comes out of the frying pan (I serve it with toast) and may also be sliced and put into sandwiches to perk up a picnic or an office lunch. It is really a kind of flat egg pancake seasoned with spring onions, coriander, green chillies, ginger and garlic. It is a good idea to have everything cut and ready before you start as this dish cooks very quickly.

1. Break the eggs into a bowl and beat well. Add a generous ¼ teaspoon salt and lots of freshly ground black pepper.

2. Put the oil in a large, non-stick frying pan and set over medium-high heat. When hot, add the spring onions. Stir and fry until the onions just start to brown at the edges. Add the garlic and stir for a few seconds. Now put in the coriander, chillies, ginger and turmeric. Stir for a few seconds. Add the lemon juice and sugar and stir to mix. Working quickly, spread the mixture around evenly in the pan.

3. Now pour in the beaten eggs and let them spread to the edges of the pan. Cover, turn the heat to medium–low and cook for a few minutes, just until the eggs have set. Cut into wedges and serve immediately.

SIMPLE SUPPERS

Raymond Blanc's

PAN-FRIED POLLOCK FILLET ON A PURÉE OF POTATOES WITH A CAPER SAUCE

SERVES
4

INGREDIENTS

50g (2oz) unsalted butter
4 × 175g (6oz) pollock fillets, skinned and boned
2 tsp lemon juice
potato purée, to serve

FOR THE CAPER SAUCE

200ml (7fl oz) chicken stock
1 fresh rosemary sprig
4 tsp small capers, washed and drained
1 tsp lemon juice
sea salt and freshly ground black pepper

We have fished cod to near extinction and while these stocks are hopefully replenishing, it is lovely to have a fish like pollock. This fish is a little underrated; it is a member of the cod family and although not as sumptuous as cod, it is still a wonderful fish with a great texture and big flavour. This dish is part of a classic French repertoire and cooked in many homes all over France.

1. Preheat the oven to 190°C/375°F/gas 5. In a non-stick ovenproof pan on medium heat, melt the butter and cook until a light golden brown colour and foaming. Fry the pollock in this for 2–3 minutes on each side to sear, until a rich golden brown. Season with a little of the lemon juice and some sea salt and black pepper. Transfer to the oven and cook for a further 5–7 minutes.

2. Use a wide spatula to remove the fish from the pan, then cover with buttered paper and leave to rest in a warm place. The resting time will allow the fish to cook right through. The residual heat will penetrate to the centre, cooking the fish perfectly. Leave the remaining cooking juices and butter in the pan.

3. To make the sauce, add the chicken stock to the juices in the pan, and boil until the sauce reaches a good consistency. Add the rosemary, simmer for 1 minute, then strain and discard the herb. Add the capers, then adjust the seasoning to taste. Lift the taste with the lemon juice. Place one portion of potato purée in the centre of each plate. Gently place the fish on top, sprinkle with a turn of black pepper and spoon the sauce around. Serve to your guests.

Rick Stein's

CRAB LINGUINE WITH PARSLEY AND CHILLI

INGREDIENTS

450g (1 lb) dried linguine or spaghetti
3 vine-ripened tomatoes, skinned,
   de-seeded and chopped
300g (11oz) fresh white crabmeat
1 tbsp freshly chopped flat-leaf parsley
1½ tbsp fresh lemon juice
50ml (2fl oz) extra-virgin olive oil
pinch of dried chilli flakes
1 garlic clove, finely chopped
salt and freshly ground black pepper

It's very important that the pasta is cooked perfectly al dente. I've suggested a cooking time of 7–8 minutes, but I always test pasta by biting it. Secondly, when I say 'warm the sauce ingredients through over a gentle heat', I really mean 'gentle' – the temperature should never get much above 60°C/140°F. Lastly, try not to break up the crabmeat if it's fresh and has been hand-picked, because lumps of crab meat folded through the pasta look very appetising.

1. Cook the pasta in a large pan of boiling, well-salted water (1 teaspoon per 600ml/1 pint) for 7–8 minutes or until it is al dente.

2. Meanwhile, put all the remaining ingredients into another pan and warm through over a gentle heat.

3. Drain the pasta, return to the pan along with the sauce and briefly toss together. Season to taste. Divide among four warmed plates and serve immediately.

Ken Hom's

RED CURRY PRAWNS

INGREDIENTS

1½ tbsp vegetable oil
3 tbsp coarsely chopped garlic
2 tbsp finely sliced shallots
2 tsp cumin seeds
1 tsp shrimp paste
1½ tbsp Thai red curry paste
1 × 400ml (14fl oz) tin coconut milk
1 tbsp Thai fish sauce (nam pla) or light
    soy sauce
2 tsp sugar
a small handful of fresh Thai basil leaves or
    ordinary basil leaves, shredded
4 kaffir lime leaves or 1 tbsp shredded
    lime zest
450g (1lb) raw prawns, shelled and
    de-veined, tails on
a handful of fresh coriander, chopped

This is a tasty version of a classic Thai dish, *gaeng phed ghoong*. Once the sauce is made, the prawns cook in just minutes. Serve with plain steamed rice.

1. Heat a wok or large frying pan until it is very hot and add the oil. When it is hot, add the garlic, shallots and cumin seeds and stir-fry for 5 minutes or until well toasted. Then add the shrimp paste and curry paste and stir-fry for another 2 minutes.

2. Now add the coconut milk, fish sauce or soy sauce, sugar, basil leaves and lime leaves or zest. Reduce the heat and simmer for 5 minutes.

3. Add the prawns and cook for 5 minutes, stirring from time to time. Add the coriander and give the mixture a good stir, then serve.

Antonio Carluccio's

LINGUINE WITH TUNA FISH SAUCE

INGREDIENTS

4 tbsp virgin olive oil

3 tbsp finely chopped fresh flat-leaf
   parsley

2 garlic cloves, finely chopped

1 small chilli, finely chopped

1cm (½in) fresh ginger, thinly sliced

450g (1lb) passata or chopped tomatoes

1 × 400g (14oz) tin tuna fish in oil, drained
   and roughly chopped

375g (13oz) linguine (fresh or dried)

salt and freshly ground black pepper

The flat, slightly rounded shape of this pasta particularly suits sauces based on fish. This recipe just goes to show how useful it is to keep a tin of tuna in the cupboard.

1. Heat the oil and gently fry 2 tablespoons of the parsley, the garlic, chilli and the ginger for a few minutes until slightly soft Add the passata or chopped tomatoes and continue to cook for another few minutes. Stir in the tuna and a little salt.

2. Meanwhile, cook the fresh or dried pasta according to the packet instructions or until al dente, and drain. Toss with the sauce and serve sprinkled with the remaining parsley and freshly ground pepper to taste.

Rick Stein's

SEARED SCALLOPS WITH NOODLES, CHILLI, GARLIC AND CORIANDER

INGREDIENTS

100g (4oz) fine dried egg noodles

2 tbsp sunflower oil

4 garlic cloves, thinly sliced

2 medium-hot red chillies, de-seeded and sliced

1cm (½in) piece of fresh ginger, cut into slivers

12 large, prepared scallops, halved horizontally

1 tsp dark soy sauce

a handful of fresh coriander, chopped

a few drops of toasted sesame oil

What I like about this recipe is the combination of cooked thin egg noodles with seared, caramelised scallops. I flavour this dish simply, with some common Chinese things like garlic, ginger, chilli and soy, and finish it with some coriander and sesame oil. It's the sort of thing they do so well in Australia and New Zealand, being close to Asia.

1. Bring a pan of lightly salted water to the boil. Add the noodles, turn off the heat and leave the noodles for 4 minutes until cooked. Drain and set aside. Add 1 tablespoon of the oil to a frying pan and heat over a medium-low heat. Add the garlic, chilli and ginger and cook for 3–4 minutes, stirring frequently, until they soften. Remove from the pan and keep to one side.

2. Heat the frying pan again until hot and add the rest of the oil. Fry the scallop slices on both sides until lightly browned – no more than 20 seconds per side. You need to do this in two batches, making sure the pan is hot between each batch.

3. Return the garlic, chilli and ginger to the pan, with the noodles and soy sauce, and stir until the noodles are well coated. Add the coriander, sesame oil and scallops, toss gently and serve.

Ken Hom's

STEAMED CANTONESE-STYLE FISH

SERVES
4

INGREDIENTS

450g (1lb) firm white fish fillets, such as
    cod or sole, skinned, or a whole fish,
    such as sole or turbot
1 tsp coarse sea salt or ordinary cooking
    salt
1½ tbsp finely shredded fresh ginger
3 tbsp finely shredded spring onions
2 tbsp light soy sauce
2 tsp dark soy sauce
1 tbsp groundnut oil
2 tsp sesame oil
fresh coriander sprigs, to garnish

Steaming is a favourite Chinese cooking method for fish. A simple but gentle technique, it doesn't mask the fresh taste of the fish, which remains moist and tender. An added bonus is that it is a very healthy way to cook. Always buy the freshest possible fish and ask your fishmonger to prepare it for cooking.

1. Pat the fish dry with kitchen paper and evenly rub with the salt, rubbing it inside the cavity as well, if you are using a whole fish. Put the fish on a heatproof plate and scatter the ginger evenly over the top.

2. Set up a steamer or put a rack into a wok or deep pan. Fill it with 5cm (2in) of water and bring to the boil over a high heat. Put the plate of fish on the rack, cover tightly and steam the fish until it is just cooked. Flat fish fillets will take about 5 minutes; whole fish, or thick fillets such as sea bass, will take 12–14 minutes. The fish should turn opaque and flake slightly, but still remain moist.

3. Remove the plate of cooked fish and pour off any liquid that may have accumulated. Scatter the spring onions on the fish, then drizzle over the light and dark soy sauces.

4. Heat the two oils together in a small saucepan until smoking, then immediately pour them over the fish. Garnish with coriander sprigs and serve at once.

 *Rick Stein's*

BROILED HADDOCK FILLETS WITH SUCCOTASH

SERVES
4

INGREDIENTS

175g (6oz) dried butter beans

100g (4oz) rindless smoked streaky bacon, in one piece

1 small onion, chopped

1 tbsp sunflower oil, if needed

300ml (10fl oz) good-quality chicken stock

3 whole corn cobs

50ml (2fl oz) double cream

4 × 175–225g (6–8oz) pieces of unskinned thick haddock fillet

15g (½oz) butter, melted

2 tbsp snipped fresh chives, plus extra to garnish

salt and freshly ground black pepper

The American word 'broiled' simply means grilled. I've kept it in to add the right atmosphere to the dish. You could also use cod, hake or kingfish. American recipes for succotash normally call for lima beans. These are the same as butter beans, one name referring to the capital of Peru, where they were first grown, and the other to their buttery, creamy texture.

1. Put the dried beans into a pan and cover with plenty of water. Bring to the boil, cover, remove from the heat and leave to soak for 2 hours.

2. Cut the bacon into 5mm (¼in) dice, put it into a pan and cook over a low heat until the fat begins to melt. Increase the heat a little and allow it to fry in its own fat until crisp and golden. Add the onion (and the sunflower oil, if it looks a little dry) and cook for about 5 minutes, until soft.

3. Drain the beans and add them to the pan, along with the stock. Simmer gently until they are just tender and the stock is well reduced. Stand the corn cobs up on a chopping board and slice away all the kernels. Add the corn to the beans, along with the cream, and simmer for 5 minutes.

4. Meanwhile, preheat the grill to high. Brush the pieces of haddock on both sides with the melted butter and season with salt and pepper. Place, skin-side up, on a lightly oiled baking sheet or the rack of the grill pan and grill for 7–8 minutes. Stir the chives into the beans and season with salt and pepper. Spoon the mixture into four warmed soup plates and place the haddock on top. Scatter over a few more chives and serve immediately.

Ken Hom's

MALAYSIAN FISH CURRY

INGREDIENTS

450g (1lb) firm white fish fillets, such as cod, halibut or sea bass, skinned

FOR THE CURRY PASTE
175g (6oz) onions, coarsely chopped
1½ tbsp finely chopped fresh ginger
1 tbsp finely chopped garlic
2 tbsp Madras curry paste
1 tsp ground coriander
½ tsp ground fennel seeds
½ tsp ground turmeric
2 tbsp lemon juice
150ml (5fl oz) tinned coconut milk

I have eaten this wonderfully fragrant curry many times in Malaysia, where fresh fish is a standard item in every home and on every restaurant menu. It makes an ideal quick meal. This savoury, delectable treat goes perfectly with plain rice.

1. Cut the fish into 5cm (2in) pieces and set aside.

2. For the curry paste, put the onions, ginger, garlic, curry paste, coriander, fennel seeds, turmeric and lemon juice in a food processor. Add half the coconut milk and blend well.

3. Pour the remaining coconut milk into a wok or saucepan and add the curry paste. Bring the mixture to a simmer and cook for 5 minutes. Add the fish pieces and cook for another 5 minutes. Serve at once.

Ainsley Harriott's

FRENCH-STYLE ROASTED COD

INGREDIENTS

450g (1lb) floury potatoes, such as Maris
  Piper, peeled and cubed
1 whole garlic bulb
4 plum tomatoes
4 sprigs of fresh rosemary
3 tbsp olive oil
4 × 150g (5oz) thick boneless cod fillets,
  skin on
4 tbsp white wine
salt and freshly ground black pepper
a handful of fresh basil leaves, to garnish

This beautifully easy, rustic-style dish is packed with flavour. Serve it at the table so your guests see it, still sizzling, in its roasting tin.

1. Preheat the oven to 220°C/425°F/gas 7. Cook the potatoes in a large pan of boiling water for 10 minutes until almost tender and starting to crumble slightly around the edges. Remove from the heat and drain well.

2. Transfer the potatoes to a large roasting tin. Break up the garlic bulb and nestle the cloves, unpeeled, among the potatoes. Roughly chop the tomatoes and scatter over the top, along with the rosemary. Season generously, then drizzle over 2 tablespoons of the olive oil. Roast for 15 minutes.

3. Add the cod fillets to the roasting tin, allowing them to rest on top of the vegetables. Drizzle the remaining oil over the top, season the fish and continue roasting for 5 minutes. Splash in the wine and cook for a further 5 minutes until the fish is just cooked. Tear over the basil leaves and serve straight from the dish. Remember to remind your guests that they'll need to peel the garlic cloves before eating them.

Rick Stein's

HARD-FRIED FISH IN RED CURRY

INGREDIENTS

2 tbsp groundnut or sunflower oil, plus
extra for deep-frying
3 tbsp Thai red curry paste (see below)
200ml (7fl oz) coconut milk
1 tbsp Thai fish sauce (nam pla)
1 tsp palm sugar or light muscovado sugar
4 × 225g (8oz) John Dory steaks
juice of ½ lime
steamed rice, to serve

Steaks of haddock, hake or salmon or even steaks of monkfish,
skinned and cut across the bone, would be a great idea too.
You could also try shark or swordfish steaks.

1. Heat the 2 tablespoons of oil in a large, deep frying pan.
    Add the red curry paste and fry for about 2 minutes, until the
    paste starts to separate from the oil. Add the coconut milk,
    fish sauce and sugar and simmer very gently for 10 minutes,
    until thickened.

2. Meanwhile, heat some oil for deep-frying to 190°C/375°F.
    Deep-fry the John Dory steaks, two at a time, for 2 minutes
    until crisp, golden and cooked through. Lift onto a baking
    sheet lined with kitchen paper and keep warm in a low oven
    while you cook the rest.

3. Once the excess oil has drained off the fish, place the steaks
    onto four warmed serving plates. Stir the lime juice into the
    sauce along with some seasoning to taste, spoon it over the fish
    and serve with some steamed rice.

TIP: To make Thai red curry paste,
roughly chop 5 large medium-hot
red chillies, 2.5cm (1in) fresh ginger,
2 lemon grass stalks (remove the
outer leaves and tough cores), 6 garlic
cloves, 3 small shallots and blend in a
food processor with 1 teaspoon each
of ground coriander, ground cumin
and salt, ¼ teaspoon of blachan (dried
shrimp paste), 2 teaspoons of paprika,
½ teaspoon of turmeric powder and
1 tablespoon of sunflower oil to form
a smooth paste.

Madhur Jaffrey's

SPICY GRILLED CHICKEN

INGREDIENTS

1 tbsp coarsely crushed black peppercorns
1 tbsp paprika (bright red, if possible)
½ tsp chilli powder, or to taste
1 tbsp garam masala
2 tsp ground cumin
2 tsp oregano
1 garlic clove, crushed
1¼ tsp salt
3 tbsp vegetable oil
2 tbsp lemon juice
2 tbsp natural yoghurt
1kg (2¼lb) jointed chicken pieces

Sometimes, after a long day at work, the easiest dish to put on the table is grilled chicken. Most Indian versions require a marinating period, but if you are rushed, as I am most of the time, follow this recipe and you will come up with delicious results – fast. The spice paste may be prepared up to a day ahead of time and refrigerated. You can also rub the chicken pieces with the spice paste and leave them for up to 24 hours before grilling. This chicken may be served, Western-style, with boiled potatoes and a green vegetable or salad. You may also serve it with rice and an Indian vegetable.

1. Preheat the grill and arrange the grilling tray at least 13–15cm (5–6in) from the source of heat. If you can control your heat, set it at medium-high. Combine all the ingredients for the spice paste in a bowl and mix well. Rub the paste over the chicken as evenly as possible.

2. Arrange the chicken pieces on the grilling tray in a single layer, with the fleshier parts up and the skin-side down. Grill for 10–12 minutes or until browned. You may need to rearrange some of the pieces, so that they all brown evenly. Turn the pieces over and cook the second side in the same way.

Ainsley Harriott's
CATALAN CHICKEN STEW WITH PEPPERS, OLIVES AND SMOKED PAPRIKA

INGREDIENTS

2 tbsp olive oil

4 chicken thighs and 2 chicken breasts,
    cut into halves

2 red onions, sliced

1 red pepper, de-seeded and sliced

2 garlic cloves, crushed

250g (9oz) chorizo sausage, diced

1 × 400g (14oz) tin chopped tomatoes

250ml (8fl oz) chicken stock

150ml (5fl oz) dry white wine

1 rounded tsp smoked paprika

a pinch of saffron (optional)

50g (2oz) raisins (optional)

2 strips orange zest

1 sprig fresh thyme

about 20 olives

1 × 400g (14oz) tin chickpeas, drained

2 tbsp chopped fresh flat-leaf parsley

salt and freshly ground black pepper

rice, to serve (see tip)

Cooking a dish in one pot not only saves on the washing up, but all the lovely flavours mingle together and the aromas are heavenly.

1. Preheat the oven to 170°C/325°F/gas 3. In a large frying pan heat 1 tablespoon of the oil. Add the chicken and brown really well all over. Transfer to a casserole.

2. Use the remaining oil to cook the onions in the frying pan until they turn golden at the edges. Add the pepper and garlic and cook for a further minute. Remove from the pan with a slotted spoon and add to the chicken. Brown the chorizo in the frying pan and add this to the chicken.

3. Pour the tomatoes, stock and wine over the chicken, and add the smoked paprika and saffron (if using). Add the raisins (if using), orange zest and thyme, season and mix well. Add the olives and chickpeas, bring to the boil, then cover and transfer to the oven for about 40 minutes. Scatter with the parsley and serve with rice.

TIP: I like to serve rice with this dish, especially Camargue red rice, which you can buy from smart delis.

Ken Hom's

CHICKEN THIGH CASSEROLE WITH ORANGE

INGREDIENTS

1½ tbsp groundnut oil
900g (2lb) skinless chicken thighs
1 tbsp finely chopped garlic
1 tbsp finely chopped fresh ginger
2 tbsp black beans, drained
2 tsp orange zest, cut into thin strips
150ml (5fl oz) fresh orange juice
2 tbsp light soy sauce
2 tsp chilli bean sauce

The Chinese buy their chickens live to ensure that they are at their freshest when cooked. Obviously, this is not practical in the West. Commercially produced chickens tend to lack taste and frozen chicken is especially bland and should be avoided whenever possible. Try to buy fresh chicken for Chinese cooking. It should have a healthy, pinkish colour, a fresh smell and be firm in texture. If possible, buy free-range or corn-fed – not only have they been raised by more humane methods, but their flavour is far superior.

1. Heat a large, heavy, flameproof casserole, then add the oil and quickly brown the chicken thighs on both sides. Push to the side of the casserole, then add the garlic, ginger, black beans and orange zest and stir for 30 seconds.

2. Add the orange juice, soy sauce and chilli bean sauce, bring to the boil, then reduce the heat to a simmer. Cover the casserole tightly and cook for 20 minutes or until the chicken is done. Check by piercing with a skewer; the juices should run clear. Serve at once.

Madhur Jaffrey's
QUICK CHICKEN KORMA (MURGH KORMA)

INGREDIENTS

4cm (1½in) piece fresh ginger, coarsely
  chopped
5–6 garlic cloves, coarsely chopped
6 tbsp vegetable oil
3 bay leaves
5cm (2in) cinnamon stick
8 cardamom pods
4 cloves
¼ tsp black cumin seeds
120g (4½oz) onions, finely chopped
1 tbsp ground coriander
1 tbsp ground cumin
3 tinned plum tomatoes, chopped
1.5kg (3lb) chicken pieces, skinned and cut
  into serving portions
¼–1 tsp chilli powder
¼ tsp salt
3 tbsp single cream

When trying to cook fast, it helps to have all the right utensils to hand. Here, a blender to make the ginger–garlic paste and a frying pan that holds all the chicken in a single layer will be of great help. This dish can be made a day ahead of time and refrigerated. It reheats well.

1. Put the ginger, garlic and 3 tablespoons water in the container of an electric blender. Blend until you have a smooth paste.

2. Put the oil in a wide frying pan or sauté pan and set over high heat. When very hot, put in the bay leaves, cinnamon, cardamom pods, cloves and cumin seeds. Stir once or twice and add the onions. Stir and fry for about 3 minutes or until the onions turn brownish. Add the paste from the blender, and the ground coriander and ground cumin, and fry for a minute. Add the chopped tomatoes and fry for another minute. Add the chicken pieces, chilli powder, salt and 250ml (8fl oz) water. Bring to the boil. Cover, turn the heat to medium and cook for 15 minutes, turning the chicken pieces over now and then.

3. Remove the cover, add the cream and cook on high heat for another 7–8 minutes or until the sauce has thickened. Stir gently as you do this.

Gizzi Erskine's
CHICKEN MEATBALL CHASSEUR WITH TAGLIATELLE

INGREDIENTS

500g (1lb 2oz) free-range chicken mince

½ tsp of mixed sea salt and freshly ground black pepper

30g (1¼oz) plain flour

2 tbsp olive oil

12 small shallots

2 garlic cloves, finely chopped

175g (6oz) chestnut mushrooms, cut into quarters

a few fresh thyme sprigs

100ml (3½ fl oz) Madeira

300ml (10fl oz) fresh chicken stock

100ml (3½ fl oz) passata

100ml (3½ fl oz) double cream

a few fresh tarragon sprigs, torn, to garnish

400g (14 oz) fresh egg tagliatelle, dressed in butter and poppy seeds, to serve

Chicken chasseur was one of the first things I ever learnt how to cook; then when I hit catering school it was one of the first things we learnt there too. I think it is a staple recipe that everyone should have under their belt. In this variation I have used meatballs and served them with buttered tagliatelle, which is not only super delicious but also reduces the cooking time so you can have it from fridge to table in 35 minutes, making it even more accessible for everyday cooking. Try it with turkey too, it's a keeper!

1. Season the minced chicken with the salt and pepper and with your hands give a really good mix breaking up the mince as you go to get all the seasoning covering the meat. Shape into small meatballs, about the size of a ping-pong ball. Coat the balls in the flour.

2. Heat a large casserole and add half the olive oil. Once hot, put in the floured chicken meatballs. Cook over a medium to high heat for 4–5 minutes, until golden brown, turning occasionally. Remove and leave to rest. You may need to do this in batches.

3. Put the rest of the olive oil in the casserole and add the shallots. Cook for 3 minutes until they begin to soften and go golden. Add the garlic and cook for 2 minutes, then add the mushrooms and thyme. Cook for a further 2 minutes. Pour in the Madeira and rub the bottom of the pan to scrape up all the flavour. Return the meatballs and add the chicken stock and passata. Bring to the boil, then reduce to a simmer and cook for 20 minutes.

4. Just before serving, add the cream to the chicken chasseur in the casserole and simmer for a further 5 minutes to reduce. Place a mound of pasta on to each plate and serve the chicken meatballs chasseur alongside. Spoon over the delicious sauce and garnish with the fresh tarragon.

Ainsley Harriott's

AROMATIC PAD THAI CHICKEN

INGREDIENTS

250g (9oz) dried flat rice noodles

2 tbsp sunflower oil

2 boneless, skinless chicken breasts, cut into 2cm (¾in) strips

1 shallot, finely sliced

2.5cm (1in) fresh ginger or galangal, finely chopped

1 lemon grass stalk, outer leaves removed and the core finely chopped

1 red bird's-eye chilli, finely chopped

2 kaffir lime leaves, finely shredded

1 garlic clove, finely chopped

4 baby pak choy, quartered

3 tbsp dark soy sauce

2 tbsp Thai fish sauce (nam pla)

juice of 1 lime, plus 1 lime for wedges, to garnish

2 tbsp sesame oil

3 tbsp chopped, roasted peanuts

a large handful of fresh coriander

I ate my best pad Thai while sitting on a very small rickety chair on a Bangkok pavement. The aroma was sensational, with the combination of all those wonderful ingredients.

1. Soak the noodles in a large bowl of boiling water for 6 minutes or as per the packet instructions. Heat the oil in a large wok or frying pan and stir-fry the chicken over a medium heat for 4–5 minutes until just starting to brown.

2. Add the shallot to the wok, along with the ginger or galangal, lemon grass, chilli, lime leaves and garlic. Mix well, then tip in the pak choy and stir-fry for a further 2 minutes. Pour the soy and fish sauces into the wok and simmer for 4 minutes until the chicken is cooked through and tender. Squeeze over the juice of 1 lime and mix well.

3. Drain the noodles and tip into the chicken, then toss and stir until well combined. Divide the pad Thai among warmed serving bowls, drizzle over a little sesame oil, a scattering of peanuts and some coriander. Serve immediately, garnished with lime wedges.

Gizzi Erskine's

JAMAICAN BROWN CHICKEN STEW

INGREDIENTS

1 tsp vegetable oil

1 medium chicken, cut into 8 portions

3 spring onions, chopped

2 onions, chopped

1 Scotch bonnet chilli, de-seeded and chopped

4 cloves garlic, chopped

a few fresh thyme sprigs

½ red pepper, de-seeded and chopped

½ green pepper, de-seeded and chopped

2 tbsp curry powder

pinch allspice mix

225g (8oz) butternut squash, peeled and cut into bite-sized cubes

200g (7oz) potatoes, peeled and cut into bite-sized cubes

600ml (1 pint) chicken stock, fresh is best

550g (1¼lb) basmati rice, cooked in coconut milk, to serve

I first got introduced to Caribbean food when I was working as a body piercer in Camden as there was an abundance of small but excellent Caribbean restaurants and takeaways in the area at the time. This classic brown chicken stew has to be one of my favourites.

1. Heat the vegetable oil in a large, deep flameproof casserole or sauté pan with a lid until really hot. Add 4–5 pieces of chicken to the oil and fry gently skin-side down for about 5 minutes on each side until the chicken is browned all over.

2. Remove the chicken from the casserole and repeat with the remaining chicken pieces. Carefully pour out most of the oil, leaving just 2 spoonfuls in the base. Add the spring onions, onions, chilli, garlic, thyme and peppers, and stir briefly. Return the chicken to the casserole with the spices, the squash and potatoes. Pour in the stock, bring to the boil and then reduce the heat, cover and simmer for 25 minutes until the liquid is reduced to a rich gravy and the chicken is cooked through. Serve with the coconut rice.

Ken Hom's

QUICK AND HEALTHY STEAMED CHICKEN

INGREDIENTS

450g (1lb) skinless, boneless chicken breasts
1 tsp coarse sea salt or ordinary cooking salt
1 tbsp light soy sauce
1 tbsp Shaoxing rice wine or dry sherry
½ tsp freshly ground white pepper
1 egg white
2 tsp cornflour
1 tsp sesame oil
1½ tsp finely shredded fresh ginger

FOR THE GARNISH
3 tbsp finely shredded spring onions
1 tbsp groundnut oil
2 tsp sesame oil

Steaming is not only a healthy way to cook food, it also brings out the subtle flavours. By keeping the food moist and cooking it slowly in warm vapours, good chicken comes out even better. Chinese cooks tend to steam the entire chicken, but when I am in a hurry I simply steam the chicken breasts. The result is a quick, but healthy, meal that takes little time to prepare. The juices from the chicken taste delicious over rice.

1. Combine the chicken with the salt, soy sauce, rice wine or dry sherry, pepper, egg white, cornflour and sesame oil. Leave to marinate for at least 20 minutes.

2. Next, set up a steamer or put a rack into a wok or deep pan and fill it with 5cm (2in) of water. Bring the water to the boil over a high heat, then reduce the heat. Put the chicken on a heatproof plate and scatter the ginger evenly over the top. Put the plate in the steamer or on the rack. Cover the pan tightly and gently steam the chicken until it is just white and firm. It will take about 8–10 minutes to cook, depending on the thickness of the breasts.

3. Remove the plate and chicken and sprinkle over the spring onions. Heat the two oils together in a small pan and, when they are hot, pour the oil mixture over the top of the chicken. Serve at once.

Gizzi Erskine's
VENISON SAUSAGE, PANCETTA AND LENTIL CASSEROLE

INGREDIENTS

1 tbsp olive oil

8 venison sausages

150g (5oz) cubed pancetta

8 medium shallots, cut in half

2 carrots, cut into chunks

8 garlic cloves, peeled but left whole

a pinch of dried chilli flakes

a fresh rosemary sprig

a few fresh thyme sprigs

1 tsp tomato purée

250g (9oz) Puy or green lentils

300ml (10fl oz) port

600ml (1 pint) fresh chicken stock

1 tsp redcurrant jelly

½ a small bunch of fresh flat-leaf parsley, roughly chopped

Venison can scare people if they are not used to eating game, but a great way of giving it a go is to have a venison sausage. In this dish, the lentils suck up all of the flavours in the pan and the sausages stay fat and juicy. This would be a cracking dish to serve up at a dinner party, and it's one of the best one-pot, great-value dishes I can think of.

1. Heat the oil in a large flameproof casserole. Add the sausages and brown them all over. Remove from the casserole then add the pancetta. Fry for a minute or two, then add the shallots, carrots and garlic cloves. Fry for about 5 minutes or until the pancetta is golden and becoming crisp and the carrots, shallots and garlic have some colour. For the last minute of cooking add the chilli flakes and herbs.

2. Add the tomato purée and cook for a further minute. Stir in the lentils, then cover with the port and stock. Bring to the boil, then reduce the heat to a simmer. Return the sausages to the casserole, cover and leave to simmer for 30 minutes or until the lentils have absorbed most of the stock. Stir in the redcurrant jelly and serve sprinkled with the chopped parsley.

Ainsley Harriott's

MEXICAN BEEF FAJITAS

INGREDIENTS

450g (1lb) rump, sirloin or fillet steak
1 red pepper
1 green pepper
1 small yellow pepper
2 large onions
150ml (5fl oz) soured cream
1 cos lettuce heart, finely shredded
3 tbsp sunflower oil
8–12 soft flour tortillas
salt and cayenne pepper

FOR THE SPICY TOMATO SALSA
1 medium-hot green chilli, de-seeded and
   finely chopped
1 small red onion, very finely chopped
1 × 200g (7oz) tin chopped tomatoes
juice of 1 lime
1 tbsp chopped fresh coriander

This is great for a Friday night supper. You can just put everything into the centre of the table and let everyone help themselves.

1. Cut the steak into long thin strips. Season well with salt and some cayenne pepper and set to one side. De-seed and thickly slice the red, green and yellow peppers. Thickly slice the onions. Preheat the grill to high.

2. Mix the salsa ingredients together with a little salt to taste. Transfer to a serving bowl. Spoon the soured cream into another bowl and the shredded lettuce into a small salad bowl.

3. Heat half the oil in a large frying pan. Add the onions, peppers and some seasoning and stir-fry over a high heat for 5 minutes until soft and slightly browned. Tip onto a plate and set aside.

4. Add half the remaining oil to the pan and, when really hot, add half the steak and stir-fry for 3–4 minutes until well browned. Set aside with the peppers while you cook the remainder.

5. Return everything to the pan and toss together briefly over a high heat. Warm the tortillas under the grill for 10 seconds. Wrap in a napkin and take to the table with the pan of steak and peppers and the bowls of salsa, lettuce and soured cream.

6. To serve, lay a tortilla on a plate and spoon some of the beef and peppers down the centre. Spoon a little spicy tomato salsa and soured cream on top, sprinkle with lettuce, then roll up tightly and eat with your hands.

Madhur Jaffrey's

BEEF OR LAMB WITH ONION AND GREEN PEPPER

INGREDIENTS

350g (12oz) cooked, boneless roast beef
  or roast lamb
1 tsp freshly ground black pepper
1¼–1½ tsp chilli powder
1 tsp ground cumin
1 tsp ground coriander
1 tsp ground turmeric
1 tsp red wine vinegar
3 tbsp vegetable oil
1 tsp cumin seeds
1 tsp black or yellow mustard seeds
10 fenugreek seeds (optional)
100g (4oz) green pepper, de-seeded and
  cut lengthways into 3mm (⅛in) slivers
150g (5oz) onions, cut into fine half-rings
1 tsp Worcestershire sauce
salt

An Anglo-Indian speciality, this calls for leftovers of cooked roast meat. Sunday's roast was invariably turned into a delicious *jhal firezi* on Mondays by many a family in cities like Calcutta. Sliced green chillies may be added to this dish at the same time as the green pepper if you want it really hot. You may serve the dish with rice, potatoes or breads.

1. Cut the cooked meat into 5mm (¼in) slices. Now stack a few slices together at a time and cut into 5mm (¼in) slivers. This does not have to be done too evenly.

2. Combine the black pepper, chilli powder, cumin, coriander, turmeric, vinegar, ½ teaspoon salt and 2 tablespoons water in a small cup. Mix and set aside.

3. Put the oil in a large frying pan over medium-high heat. When hot, add the cumin, mustard and fenugreek seeds (if using). As soon as the mustard seeds begin to pop, add the green pepper and onions. Stir and fry until the onions have browned quite a bit and the mass of vegetables has reduced. Sprinkle about ⅛ teaspoon salt over the top and stir. Add the meat and the spice mixture from the cup. Stir rapidly on the same medium-high heat for a minute or so until the meat has heated through. Add the Worcestershire sauce and stir to mix.

Ainsley Harriott's
CORNED BEEF HASH WITH POACHED EGG

INGREDIENTS

550g (1¼lb) potatoes, cut into 1cm
 (½in) cubes
2 tbsp olive oil
1 large onion, chopped
knob of butter
1 × 200g (7oz) tin corned beef, cut into
 1cm (½in) cubes
2 tbsp chopped fresh flat-leaf parsley
salt and freshly ground black pepper
tomato ketchup, to serve

FOR THE POACHED EGGS
1 tbsp white wine vinegar
½ tsp salt
2 very fresh eggs

Originally from the southern states of the USA, this terrific comfort food can also be served with a fried egg and a good dollop of tomato ketchup on the side.

1. Place the potatoes in a pan and cover with boiling water. Add a pinch of salt and bring to the boil, then cover and simmer for 5 minutes.

2. Meanwhile, heat the oil in a large, heavy-based, non-stick frying pan. Add the onion and sauté for 3–4 minutes until softened. Drain the potatoes, then add the butter to the onion mixture. Once it is foaming, tip in the potatoes, season and sauté for 8–10 minutes until the potatoes are crisp and golden.

3. To poach the eggs, heat 4cm (1½in) water in a large, deep frying pan until little bubbles begin to appear on the surface. Add 1 tablespoon white wine vinegar and ½ teaspoon salt. Break each egg into a teacup, then slide it gently into the water. Cook for 3½ minutes, making sure the water stays at a very gentle simmer. Life them out of the water with a slotted spoon and drain briefly on kitchen paper.

4. Meanwhile, add the corned beef to the potato and onion mixture and continue to sauté for a further 3–4 minutes until the corned beef has broken down and crisped up in places. Stir in the parsley and season to taste. Serve on warmed plates with a poached egg on top, with tomato ketchup.

Ken Hom's

VIETNAMESE-STYLE BEEF STEW

INGREDIENTS

6 lemon grass stalks

1.5kg (3lb) stewing beef, such as brisket

1 small onion

4 spring onions

450g (1lb) carrots

2 tbsp groundnut oil

6 slices fresh ginger

6 garlic cloves, lightly crushed

2–3 tsp crushed dried red chilli

coarsely chopped fresh basil and mint, to
garnish

FOR THE BRAISING SAUCE

900ml (1½ pints) home-made chicken
stock (see page 10) or good-quality
bought stock

75g (3oz) sugar

3 tbsp light soy sauce

2 tbsp dark soy sauce

3 tbsp Shaoxing rice wine or dry sherry

4 star anise

2 tsp five-spice powder

2 tbsp tomato purée

2 tsp salt

1 tsp freshly ground black pepper

This hearty dish is perfect for a cold winter's night. It takes a little time to cook, but can happily bubble away while you get on with other things.

1. Peel off the tough outer layers of the lemon grass stalks, leaving the tender, whitish centre. Crush with the flat of a knife, then cut into 7.5cm (3in) pieces. Cut the beef into 5cm (2in) cubes. Coarsely chop the onion and cut the spring onions on a slight diagonal into 5cm (2in) lengths. Peel the carrots and cut them on a slight diagonal into 5cm (2in) lengths.

2. Heat a wok or large frying pan, add the oil and, when it is very hot and slightly smoking, add half the beef. Fry for about 10 minutes, until browned all over, then remove with a slotted spoon and set aside. Repeat with the remaining beef.

3. Pour off most of the excess oil from the wok, leaving about 2 tablespoons. Add the lemon grass, onion, spring onions, ginger, garlic and dried chilli and stir-fry for 5 minutes. Transfer this mixture to a large casserole or saucepan. Add the browned beef and all the ingredients for the braising sauce. Bring to the boil, skim off any fat from the surface, then reduce the heat to a low simmer. Cover and braise for 1½–2 hours.

4. Add the carrots and continue to cook for 30 minutes, until the beef and carrots are tender. Remove the beef and carrots with a slotted spoon and set aside. Turn the heat up to high and boil the liquid rapidly for about 15 minutes, until reduced and slightly thickened. Garnish with the chopped basil and mint and serve immediately. The stew can also be left to cool and then reheated later, garnished and served.

Antonio Carluccio's

BOLOGNESE SAUCE

INGREDIENTS

25g (1oz) butter
2 tbsp olive oil
1 medium-sized onion, chopped
250g (9oz) minced beef
250g (9oz) minced pork
6 tbsp white wine
1 tsp concentrated tomato purée
1kg (2¼lb) passata or chopped tomatoes
salt and freshly ground black pepper

TO SERVE

freshly cooked tagliatelle
freshly grated Parmesan (optional)

One of the best-known Italian recipes abroad, spaghetti Bolognese does not exist in Italy. It is something you will find in a restaurant run by non-Italians or by Italians not in touch with genuine Italian food. The real thing is called tagliatelle *al ragù* and comes from Bologna in Emilia Romagna. Genuine *ragù Bolognese* is a combination of at least two types of meat, like lean minced beef and pork, plus oil and butter, a little wine, an onion, plump ripe tomatoes and tomato paste. The sprinkling of freshly grated Parmesan perfectly crowns this very Emilian dish.

1. Heat the butter and oil in a pan and fry the chopped onion. Then add the meat and fry until golden brown. Stir in the wine, tomato purée and passata or chopped tomatoes. Season with salt and pepper to taste. Cover with a lid and leave to simmer for about 2 hours, stirring from time to time. Serve with freshly cooked tagliatelle and sprinkle with freshly grated Parmesan, if desired, but purists like this dish without.

MINCED LAMB WITH TOMATOES AND PEAS

SERVES
4–6

INGREDIENTS

100g (4oz) onions
5cm (2in) piece fresh ginger
5–6 large garlic cloves
4 tbsp vegetable oil
½ tsp chilli powder
1 tsp cumin seeds
1 tsp coriander seeds
½ tsp turmeric powder
200g (7oz) tomatoes, chopped
4 tbsp natural yoghurt
550 g (1¼lb) minced lamb
1¼ tsp salt
2 tsp garam masala
2 tbsp lemon juice
1 fresh hot green chilli, chopped
6 tbsp coarsely chopped fresh coriander
150g (5oz) peas, fresh or frozen

Here I have used a quick method to chop the onion, garlic and ginger finely. I put them into a food processor and used the 'pulse' method rapidly starting and stopping the machine until I have the result I want.

1. Coarsely chop the onions, ginger and garlic, then put them into the container of a food processor and chop finely.

2. Put the oil in a wide, non-stick pan and set over a medium-high heat. When hot, put in the finely chopped mixture from the food processor. Stir and fry until it is somewhat brown. Add the chilli powder, cumin seeds, coriander seeds and turmeric. Stir once or twice. Now add the tomatoes and natural yoghurt. Stir on high heat until the tomatoes are soft. Add the meat, salt and garam masala. Stir, breaking up any lumps, for 2 minutes. Add 250ml (8fl oz) water. Stir and bring to a simmer. Cover, turn the heat to low and simmer for 25 minutes.

3. Add the lemon juice, green chilli, fresh coriander and peas. Stir and bring to a simmer. Cover the pan and cook on low heat for 10 minutes.

Ken Hom's

HOT AND TANGY MINCED LAMB

INGREDIENTS

1 tbsp groundnut oil

450g (1lb) minced lamb

3 tbsp coarsely chopped garlic

2 tbsp coarsely chopped fresh ginger

2 tbsp tomato paste

2 tbsp sesame paste

1½ tbsp dark soy sauce

1 tbsp lemon juice

1 tbsp chilli bean sauce

2 tsp sugar

1 tbsp Shaoxing rice wine or dry sherry

This dish, in which the flavours of East and West meet, readily combines with pasta, rice, noodles or even bread to make an easy and substantial meal in less than 30 minutes. You can use minced beef instead of lamb, if you prefer. Sesame paste is a rich, thick, creamy brown paste made from roasted sesame seeds and should not be confused with the Middle Eastern tahini. If you cannot find sesame paste, use smooth peanut butter.

1. Heat a wok or large frying pan until very hot, then add the oil and lamb. Stir-fry for 2 minutes, then add the garlic and ginger and cook for another minute.

2. Stir in the tomato paste, sesame paste, soy sauce, lemon juice, chilli bean sauce, sugar and rice wine or sherry. Cook for 4 minutes, then serve.

TIP: You will find it quicker if, as in this recipe, you are required to add a number of ingredients at the same time, you measure them together into a bowl and add them all at once.

LIGHTNING LAMB DHANSAK

INGREDIENTS

500g (1lb 2oz) cubed lamb
2 tbsp garam masala
2–3 tbsp vegetable oil
2 onions, thinly sliced
2 garlic cloves, thinly sliced
200g (7oz) diced pumpkin or squash
100g (4oz) dried red lentils
600ml (1 pint) hot vegetable stock
1 tbsp curry paste
1 tbsp tamarind paste
25g (1oz) caster sugar
2 tbsp chopped fresh mint or coriander
juice of 1 lemon
salt and freshly ground black pepper
pilau rice, to serve

Lamb dhansak is one of the most popular dishes on any Indian menu and absolutely delicious. For complete authenticity, it can take a whole day to make the dish, but this lightning version combines all the flavours and tastes superb. Tamarind paste is available in large supermarkets or good delis.

1. Toss the lamb in the garam masala. Heat 1 tablespoon of the oil in a large pan and brown the lamb briefly. Transfer to a plate and set aside.

2. Add the remaining oil to the pan, then add the onions, garlic and pumpkin or squash and cook for 5 minutes until softened and beginning to brown.

3. Now add the lentils, stock, curry paste, tamarind paste and sugar and stir the lamb back into the pan. Bring to the boil, cover, reduce the heat and simmer for 25–30 minutes, stirring occasionally, until the mixture is thickened and the ingredients are lovely and tender. Check the seasoning, then stir in the mint or coriander and lemon juice, to taste. Serve with pilau rice.

Antonio Carluccio's

PAPPARDELLE WITH MEAT SAUCE

INGREDIENTS

6 tbsp olive oil
1 small onion, finely chopped
1 celery stick, finely chopped
1 carrot, peeled and finely chopped
200g (7oz) minced pork (or use skinned
   100 per cent pork sausages)
200g (7oz) lean minced beef
150ml (5fl oz) dry red wine
3 tbsp tomato purée diluted with 2 tbsp
   warm water
2 bay leaves
150ml (5fl oz) stock
450g (1lb) pappardelle (fresh or dried)
75g (3oz) freshly grated Parmesan
salt and freshly ground black pepper

Pappardelle is a very satisfying pasta indeed, especially when it is accompanied by a meat sauce. This pasta is eaten in Italy whenever a roast is made, with the meat sediment from the roasting tin forming the basis of the sauce. In this recipe I have given you a quicker version.

1. Heat the oil and gently fry the onion, celery and carrot until soft. Add the pork and beef, and continue frying until the meat is browned. Pour in the wine and let it evaporate for 1–2 minutes. Add the tomato purée with the water, and the bay leaves. Cook for another 10 minutes. Stir in the stock, add salt and pepper to taste, and heat through for 1–2 minutes. Remove the bay leaves.

2. Cook the pasta for 5–7 minutes or until al dente. Drain and serve with the meat sauce, and sprinkle with grated Parmesan.

Ainsley Harriott's
SOUTHERN-STYLE SAUSAGE JAMBALAYA

INGREDIENTS

2 tbsp sunflower oil

100g (4oz) chorizo, thickly sliced

1 × 225g (8oz) smoked pork sausage ring, thickly sliced

4 garlic cloves, crushed

1 medium onion, chopped

1 red pepper, de-seeded and cut into chunky strips

1 green pepper, de-seeded and cut into chunky strips

2 celery sticks, sliced

1 tsp chilli powder

1 tsp hot paprika

225g (8oz) long-grain rice

1 tsp fresh thyme

2 bay leaves

400ml (14fl oz) passata

300ml (10fl oz) chicken stock

225g (8oz) large cooked, peeled prawns

2 tbsp fresh flat-leaf parsley, chopped

4 spring onions, thinly sliced

salt and cayenne pepper

This tasty Cajun dish is perfect fork-food for dinner in front of the telly.

1. Heat the sunflower oil in a large, deep frying pan. Fry the chorizo and smoked pork sausage slices on both sides until golden. Lift out and set aside.

2. Add the garlic to the pan, along with the onion, red and green peppers and celery, and fry for 5 minutes until they are all lightly browned. Add the chilli powder and paprika and cook for 1 minute. Stir in the browned sausages, the rice, thyme, bay leaves, passata, chicken stock, a good sprinkling of salt and some cayenne pepper. Bring to the boil, cover and reduce the heat, and simmer gently for 20 minutes.

3. Tip the prawns into the pan, cover and cook for a further 4–5 minutes. Uncover and fork the prawns and the parsley into the rice. Scatter over the spring onions and serve immediately.

Gizzi Erskine's

TALEGGIO AND SAGE-STUFFED PORK CHOPS WITH ROASTED APPLES

INGREDIENTS

4 Braeburn apples, halved and cored

50g (2oz) butter, plus 8 tsp

a handful fresh sage leaves

1 tsp golden caster sugar

4 × 225g (8oz) pork loin chops, French trimmed (ask your butcher to do this for you)

150g (5oz) Taleggio cheese, cut into 4 long, thin slices

sea salt and freshly ground black pepper

You don't get much more British than pork chops, sage and apple! So, I thought I'd throw some Taleggio cheese into the mix. The cheesy melting middle is a scrummy surprise, and the whole thing is drenched in sage butter for some Anglo-Italian magic. Swap the apples for pears and you've got another great dish.

1. Preheat the oven to 200°C/400°F/gas 6. Place the apple halves on a roasting tin, cut-side up, and place 1 teaspoon of butter on each. Pop a couple of sage leaves on top, and sprinkle with the sugar. Bake for 20 minutes until soft in the middle and crisp and caramelised on the outside.

2. Meanwhile, slice a pocket into each pork chop along the edge that doesn't have the bone, slicing fairly deeply into the chop, about three-quarters of the way through. Stuff each chop with a slice of Taleggio and a couple more sage leaves. Season with lots of salt and pepper.

3. Heat half of the remaining butter in a frying pan over a high heat and add the rest of the sage. When it's really hot (but not so hot that it begins to burn), add the chops and fry for 2 minutes. Turn the chops over, add the last of the butter and cook for a further 2 minutes. Transfer the chops to the same roasting tin as the apples. Pour over the sage butter and roast for a further 5 minutes.

4. Remove the tin from the oven and leave to rest for 5 minutes. By now the chops will be oozing with melting cheese. Serve each chop with 2 apple halves and some of the buttery juices poured over.

Ken Hom's

SICHUAN-STYLE PORK WITH PEANUTS

SERVES
4

INGREDIENTS

450g (1lb) lean boneless pork
1½ tbsp groundnut oil
1 dried red chilli, split lengthways
6 tbsp raw peanuts

FOR THE MARINADE
1 tbsp light soy sauce
2 tsp Shaoxing rice wine or dry sherry
1 tsp sesame oil
2 tsp cornflour

FOR THE SAUCE
2 tbsp home-made chicken stock (see page 10) or good-quality bought stock, or water
2 tbsp Shaoxing rice wine or dry sherry
1 tbsp dark soy sauce
2 tsp sugar
1 tbsp chopped garlic
1½ tbsp finely chopped spring onions
2 tsp finely chopped fresh ginger
1 tbsp Chinese black rice vinegar or cider vinegar
1 tsp salt
1 tsp sesame oil

This is a pork version of a classic Sichuan Chinese dish that is usually made with chicken. It is quick and easy to prepare and is quite savoury – as is to be expected from any Sichuan recipe. Serve with plain rice and another vegetable dish for a complete meal.

1. Cut the pork into 2.5cm (1in) cubes and put them in a bowl. Add all the marinade ingredients, mix well and leave to marinate for 10 minutes.

2. Heat a wok or large frying pan over a high heat. Add the groundnut oil and, when it is hot and slightly smoking, add the chilli and stir-fry for a few seconds (you may remove it when it turns black or leave it in; leaving it in will make the flavour stronger).Add the peanuts and stir-fry them for 1 minute. Remove the peanuts from the wok and set aside.

3. Lift the pork from the marinade with a slotted spoon, add to the wok and stir-fry for 3 minutes or until lightly browned. Remove and drain in a colander set inside a bowl.

4. Wipe the wok clean and add all the sauce ingredients, except the sesame oil. Bring to the boil and then reduce the heat. Return the pork to the wok and cook for about 2 minutes, mixing well all the time.

5. Finally, return the peanuts to the wok and add the sesame oil. Give the mixture a good stir and serve immediately.

Gizzi Erskine's
STILTON RISOTTO WITH SAUSAGE, SPRING GREENS AND CRISPY SAGE

SERVES
4

INGREDIENTS

4 Italian pork sausages with fennel
2 tbsp olive oil
1 tbsp butter
1 onion, finely chopped
3 garlic cloves, finely chopped
400g (14oz) risotto rice
1 glass white wine
750ml (1¼ pints) hot chicken or vegetable stock
1 small head of spring greens, outer leaves and stalks removed, then finely sliced
100g (4oz) Stilton cheese
a handful of fresh sage leaves

A great, sociable dish to make while nattering to your friends.

1. Remove the sausages from their skins. Heat one tablespoon of oil and the butter in a heavy-bottomed pan and add the sausages to the pan, breaking them up with a wooden spoon so they resemble small meatballs. It doesn't matter if some of the sausages break up too much; it simply adds to the whole texture. When the sausage is browned remove from the pan with a slotted spoon and drain out any excess oil so there is only about 1 tablespoon left in the pan.

2. Add the onions and fry over a lowish heat for 10 minutes or until they have softened. For the last minute of cooking add the garlic to the pan.

3. Add the rice and stir for a minute or two to coat the grains. Pour over the glass of wine and keep stirring while the wine is absorbed into the grain. Gradually ladle the hot stock into the risotto letting it absorb between each ladleful. Keep stirring it, too, as this encourages the starch to come out, which is what makes risotto have that creamy texture.

4. With your last three ladlefuls of stock add in the spring greens. The rice is ready when the grains are cooked but still have a little bite and the rice is loose but not soupy. Add in the Stilton, and watch the risotto become rich and velvety.

5. In a separate, small frying pan, heat the remaining oil. Add the sage leaves and fry for a minute or two until crisp. Serve the risotto with a scattering of sage leaves.

Antonio Carluccio's

SPAGHETTI CARBONARA

INGREDIENTS

500g (1lb 2oz) spaghetti or spaghettoni
   (the largest spaghetti) (fresh or dried)
25g (1oz) lard
25g (1oz) butter
2 tbsp olive oil
1 garlic clove, slightly squashed
100g (4oz) pancetta or guanciale, cut into
   small chunks
5 tbsp dry white wine
5 eggs
100g (4oz) freshly grated Parmesan (or
   pecorino cheese for the purists)
3 tbsp finely chopped fresh flat-leaf
   parsley
salt and freshly ground black pepper

I include a recipe for this well-known dish because most people I know get it completely wrong, either adding milk or cream or letting the eggs become scrambled. This recipe is the real thing. It was brought to Lazio from Umbria by coal men (*carbonari*), who came to sell charcoal to the Romans. Since then it has been adopted by the Romans and is famous all over the world.

1. Cook the pasta in a large pan of boiling salted water according to the packet instructions or until al dente. Meanwhile, heat the lard, butter and oil in a pan and fry the garlic and pancetta or guanciale until crisp. Discard the garlic and add the white wine to the pan. Boil to evaporate it a little.

2. Lightly beat the eggs in a large bowl with the grated Parmesan, parsley and some salt and pepper. When the pasta is ready, drain and add to the egg mixture in the bowl, stirring to coat the pasta. Then add to the pancetta or guanciale in the pan. Stir a couple of times and then serve.

Caution: This recipe contains lightly cooked eggs.

Madhur Jaffrey's

MUSHROOM CURRY

INGREDIENTS

4cm (1½in) piece fresh ginger, chopped
100g (4oz) onions, chopped
3 garlic cloves, chopped
450g (1lb) large mushrooms
6 tbsp vegetable oil
3 tbsp natural yoghurt
1 tsp tomato purée
2 tsp ground coriander
¼ tsp salt
⅛–¼ tsp chilli powder
2 tbsp chopped fresh coriander

I have used ordinary white mushrooms here but you may make this with almost any seasonal mushrooms. Whichever kind you get, cut them into large, chunky pieces so they do not get lost in the sauce.

1. Put the ginger, onion and garlic into the container of an electric blender along with 3 tablespoons water and blend until smooth. Wipe the mushrooms with a damp cloth and cut them into halves or quarters, depending upon size.

2. Put 3 tablespoons of the oil in a non-stick frying pan and set over high heat. When hot, put in the mushrooms. Stir and fry for 2–3 minutes or until the mushrooms have lost their raw look. Empty the contents of the pan into a bowl. Wipe the pan.

3. Put the remaining oil into the pan and set over high heat. When hot, add the paste from the blender. Stir and fry for 3–4 minutes until it starts turning brown. Add 1 tablespoon of the yoghurt and fry for 30 seconds. Add another tablespoon of yoghurt and fry for 30 seconds. Do this a third time. Now add the tomato purée and fry for 30 seconds. Add the ground coriander and stir once or twice. Now put in 300ml (10fl oz) water, the mushrooms and their juices, salt and chilli powder. Stir and bring to a simmer. Turn the heat to low and simmer for 5 minutes. Sprinkle the fresh coriander over the top before serving.

Gizzi Erskine's
BRIGHT GREEN PEA AND GOATS' CHEESE RISOTTO

SERVES
4

INGREDIENTS

600g (1¼lb) frozen peas
a small bunch fresh mint
1 tbsp olive oil
2 leeks, finely chopped
400g (14oz) arborio rice
1 glass white wine
600ml (1 pint) hot chicken or vegetable
    stock
1 tsp white truffle oil, plus extra to serve
1 tbsp freshly grated Parmesan, plus extra
    to serve
a knob of butter
2 tbsp crème fraîche
grated zest and juice of a lemon
1 log goats' cheese
1 punnet of pea shoots
salt and freshly ground black pepper

This risotto is bright green as it has puréed peas running through it. I would always use frozen peas as they are so much sweeter and really add depth to the dish. The truffle oil is optional, but it's a great store-cupboard ingredient and makes a really sexy addition to loads of dishes.

1. Cook the peas in some water with the mint. When cooked, drain 400g (14oz) of the peas, saving the rest, and blitz in a blender with the mint to a smooth green purée. Keep the peas warm.

2. Heat the oil in a large, heavy-based saucepan over a low heat. Add the leeks and sauté about 5 minutes. Add the rice and toast in the hot oil for 1 minute. Add the wine and stir until absorbed. Add one ladleful of the hot stock, adjust the heat to maintain a gentle simmer, and cook, stirring continuously, until the liquid is absorbed. Continue adding the stock, one ladleful at a time and stirring continuously, until the rice is just tender but slightly firm in the centre and the mixture is creamy – this takes about 20 minutes.

3. Now add the mushy peas, whole peas, truffle oil, Parmesan, butter and crème fraîche and stir in quickly. Taste and season if needed. Add the lemon zest and juice. Stir in the goats' cheese until it is molten and melting throughout the risotto. Top with the pea shoots, more Parmesan and truffle oil, and serve.

Antonio Carluccio's

PENNE WITH CHILLI SAUCE

INGREDIENTS

6 tbsp olive oil

2 garlic cloves, finely chopped

2 red chillies, finely chopped

1 × 400g (14oz) tin chopped tomatoes or
450g (1lb) passata

2 tbsp finely chopped fresh flat-leaf
parsley

375g (13oz) dried penne or penne rigate

salt

A fantastic dish for a quick meal on the run, this fiery sauce takes only moments to cook. If you want a milder meal, remove the seeds from the chillies when you chop them.

1. Heat the oil and briefly fry the garlic and the chillies. Add the chopped tomatoes or passata and cook for a few minutes, then add the parsley and salt to taste.

2. Cook the pasta in boiling salted water according to the packet instructions or until al dente, then drain. Add the pasta to the sauce and toss together.

Madhur Jaffrey's

EASY CHICKPEA CURRY

INGREDIENTS

350g (12oz) drained weight tinned
   chickpeas (from a 540g can)
2 tomatoes, about 225g (8oz)
5cm (2in) piece fresh ginger
4 garlic cloves
3–6 fresh hot green chillies
25g (1oz) fresh coriander
1 tbsp ground coriander
2 tsp ground cumin
½ tsp ground turmeric
½ tsp cayenne pepper
salt
2 medium potatoes, about 255g (8oz),
   peeled
150g (5oz) onions
3 tbsp corn, peanut or olive oil
1 medium cinnamon stick
5 whole cardamom pods
2 bay leaves

I often make this spicy, North India-style curry, as it cooks easily and quickly. I use tinned chickpeas and, although it looks like a long list of seasonings, they actually all grind together in one go in the blender.

1. Leave the chickpeas to drain in a colander.

2. Chop the tomatoes, ginger, garlic, chillies and fresh coriander and put in a blender with the ground coriander, cumin, turmeric, cayenne pepper, 1 teaspoon salt and 5–6 tablespoons water. Blend until smooth, pushing down with a rubber spatula when necessary.

3. Cut the potatoes into 2cm (¾in) dice. Finely chop the onions. Pour the oil into a wide, medium, lidded pan and set over a medium-high heat. When the oil is hot, add the cinnamon, cardamom and bay leaves. Ten seconds later, add the onions and potatoes. Stir and fry for about 6 minutes or until the onions are lightly browned. Add the paste from the blender. Stir for a minute. Cover, reduce the heat to medium-low, and cook for 6–7 minutes, lifting the lid now and then to stir. Add the chickpeas, ¼ teaspoon salt and 250ml (8fl oz) water. Stir and bring to a simmer. Cover, and cook gently on a low heat for 20 minutes, stirring occasionally.

Ainsley Harriott's

TOMATO, FETA AND BASIL PIZZA

SERVES
4

INGREDIENTS

1 × 145g pack pizza-base mix
2 tbsp roughly chopped fresh mixed
  herbs (e.g. basil, rosemary, flat-leaf
  parsley)
100ml (3½fl oz) hand-hot water
2 plum tomatoes, cut into wedges
8 firm vine-ripened tomatoes, cut into
  chunks
120g (4½oz) cherry tomatoes, halved
1 red onion, cut into thin wedges
75g (3oz) feta cheese, crumbled
salt and freshly ground black pepper
fresh basil leaves, to garnish

This quick and easy pizza is great to have ready for the kids to eat when they get home from school. You can spice it up with other low-fat toppings: try par-boiling courgettes and adding them along with some caramelised onions. When the pizza is cooked, scatter with fresh basil leaves.

1. Preheat the oven to 220°C/425°F/gas 7, putting a large baking sheet inside to heat at the same time. Mix together the pizza-base mix, herbs and water to form a soft dough. Knead lightly on a lightly floured surface until the dough is smooth. Roll out to about a 25cm (10in) circle.

2. Lift the pizza circle onto the preheated baking sheet and scatter over the tomatoes, onion and feta. Season and bake for 20 minutes until golden. Scatter over the basil leaves to garnish.

TIP: You could use some fresh peppery rocket instead of basil as a garnish.

TORTIGLIONI WITH MUSHROOMS AND CHEESE

INGREDIENTS

20g (¾oz) dried ceps

6 tbsp olive oil

200g (7oz) button mushrooms, finely sliced

200g (7oz) ricotta cheese, crumbled

100g (4oz) coarsely grated fontina cheese

50g (2oz) freshly grated pecorino cheese

3 eggs, lightly beaten

375g (13oz) dried tortiglioni or fusilli

salt and freshly ground black pepper

Tortiglioni is one of the larger pastas that looks like a twisted, hollow macaroni. Sometimes it goes by other names such as *ricciolo*, fusilli or *eliceh*. It is usually good with tomato-based sauces, but I would like you to try this exception. This sauce looks untidy, but tastes delicious.

1. Soak the ceps in warm water for 20 minutes. Drain, reserving the soaking water. Squeeze the ceps dry and then finely chop.

2. Heat the oil and gently fry the button mushrooms. Add the ceps with 2–3 tablespoons of the reserved soaking water and cook for 5 minutes. Remove from the heat and gently stir in the ricotta, fontina and pecorino cheeses and the beaten eggs. (The eggs should not be cooked but remain liquid at this stage.) Taste and add salt, if necessary, and pepper.

3. Cook the pasta in boiling salted water for 6–7 minutes or until al dente, then drain. Return the pasta to the pan and mix well with the sauce, so that the egg just starts to thicken with the heat of the pasta. Serve immediately.

Caution: This recipe contains lightly cooked eggs.

Ken Hom's

MALAYSIAN VEGETABLE CURRY

INGREDIENTS

2 × 400ml (14fl oz) tins coconut milk

100g (4oz) onion, finely sliced

1 tbsp finely chopped garlic

½ tsp shrimp paste

½ tsp ground turmeric

2 fresh red or green chillies, de-seeded and sliced

1 tsp salt

½ tsp freshly ground black pepper

175g (6oz) potatoes, peeled and thickly sliced

350g (12oz) Chinese leaves (Peking cabbage), shredded

1 tbsp lemon juice

Although one can detect an Indian influence in this typical Malaysian dish, the flavours are unique. What makes a great difference is the use of shrimp paste, an aromatic seasoning found in many Malaysian vegetable dishes. When it is combined with chillies, the results are sensational. There is a secret, however, to this recipe: do not add all the vegetables at the same time. Like stir-frying, stewing requires you to give different vegetables different cooking times. If the cooking times are properly observed, the whole dish comes out perfectly done.

1. Pour the coconut milk into a wok or large frying pan and bring to a simmer. Add the onion, garlic, shrimp paste, turmeric, chillies, salt and pepper and return to a simmer.

2. Add the potatoes and cook for 8 minutes, until they are almost tender, then add the Chinese leaves. Cover and simmer for 6 minutes, until they are thoroughly cooked. Stir in the lemon juice and serve immediately.

SWEET
TREATS
AND
PUDS

Ainsley Harriott's

CHOCOLATE AND PEAR UPSIDE-DOWN PUD

INGREDIENTS

75g (3oz) unsalted butter, softened
75g (3oz) caster sugar
4 ripe but firm dessert pears, such as
  Williams
juice of 1 lemon
6 double-chocolate muffins
crème fraîche, to serve

This is the ultimate cheat's pud because it uses ready-made muffins, but is none the worse for that.

1. Pre-heat the oven to 200°C/400°F/gas 6. Thickly smear the bottom of a 20cm (8in) ovenproof frying pan with the butter and sprinkle over the sugar.

2. Peel the pears, cut them into halves or quarters and remove the cores. Put them in a bowl and toss them with the lemon juice to stop them from going brown. Drain off any excess juice, then tip them into the prepared frying pan. Place over a medium heat and cook for 7–10 minutes, shaking the pan occasionally to stop the pears from sticking, until the butter and sugar caramelise and turn toffee-coloured and the pears are just tender. You might need to lower the heat a little, depending on how quickly the pears are cooking.

3. Crumble the chocolate muffins into small pieces and scatter them evenly over the pears. Cover with an ovenproof plate or the base of a flan tin, press down gently to bind everything together slightly, and leave the plate in place. Transfer to the oven and bake for 10 minutes, or until the pears are completely tender but still holding their shape.

4. Remove the frying pan from the oven and leave the pudding to cool for 30 minutes so that all the juices have time to be well absorbed and the caramel can set slightly.

5. To serve, remove the plate and loosen the edges of the pudding with a round-bladed knife. Cover the top of the pan with an inverted serving plate, take hold of both the plate and the pan, then turn them over together. Remove the frying pan, checking to see that the pudding is now on the plate, and serve cut into wedges with a spoonful of crème fraîche.

Mary Berry's

EASY LEMON CHEESECAKE

INGREDIENTS

FOR THE BASE
10 digestive biscuits
50g (2oz) butter
25g (1oz) demerara sugar

FOR THE FILLING
150ml (5fl oz) single cream
1 × 397g (14oz) tin full-fat condensed milk
175g (6oz) low-fat soft cheese
grated zest and juice of 3 large lemons
fresh strawberries, hulled and halved,
   to decorate

A quick cheesecake that's always popular with my family.

1. Put the biscuits into a plastic bag and crush with a rolling pin. Melt the butter in a medium-sized pan. Remove the pan from the heat and stir in the biscuit crumbs and sugar. Press evenly over the base and sides of the flan dish, then leave to set.

2. To make the filling, mix together the cream, condensed milk, soft cheese and lemon zest, then add the lemon juice a little at a time, whisking until the mixture thickens.

3. Pour the mixture into the flan case and leave to chill in the fridge for 3–4 hours or overnight. Decorate with a few fresh, hulled and halved strawberries.

EQUIPMENT NEEDED: a 23cm (9in) flan dish

STICKY APRICOT PUDDING

INGREDIENTS

175g (6oz) self-raising flour
1 level tsp baking powder
50g (2oz) caster sugar
50g (2oz) butter, softened, plus extra for
   greasing
1 large egg
grated zest of 1 lemon
150ml (5fl oz) milk
1 × 410g (14oz) tin apricot halves (or other
   tinned fruit), drained
crème fraîche, whipped cream, ice cream
   or custard, to serve

FOR THE TOPPING
50g (2oz) butter, melted
175g (6oz) demerara sugar

> EQUIPMENT NEEDED: a 28cm
> (11in) shallow ovenproof baking dish

> TIP: You can replace the apricots with
> whatever fruit you have to hand. Both
> sliced dessert and cooking apples work
> well. Arrange the apple slices evenly
> over the top of the sponge mixture.
> Other good alternatives are rhubarb
> and plums. Cut the plums in half and
> remove the stones, then arrange them
> cut-side down.

This is a very adaptable recipe and one of my family's favourites. You can use a variety of different fruits, either fresh or canned. It's a good dessert to serve for Sunday lunch. Just place the pudding on the top shelf, above the roast, and let it cook there. It couldn't be easier.

1. Preheat the oven to 230°C/450°F/gas 8. Butter the ovenproof baking dish.

2. Measure the flour, baking powder, sugar, butter, egg, lemon zest and milk into a large bowl. Beat together until the mixture forms a soft, cake-like consistency.

3. Spread the mixture into the prepared baking dish and arrange the apricots, cut-side down, over the top. Brush or drizzle the melted butter for the topping over the apricots, then sprinkle with the demerara sugar.

4. Bake in the preheated oven for 35 minutes or until the top has caramelised to a deep golden brown. Serve warm, with crème fraîche, whipped cream, ice cream or even hot custard on a cold winter's day.

Raymond Blanc's

POACHED PEARS WITH CASSIS COULIS

SERVES
4

INGREDIENTS

4 ripe pears, about 175g (6oz) each (use
   Guyot or Williams)
1 litre (1¾ pints) water
200g (7oz) caster sugar
½ vanilla pod
juice of ½ lemon

FOR THE BLACKCURRANT COULIS

1 litre (1¾ pints) water
250g (9oz) fresh blackcurrants (weighed
   after picking from stalks)
50g (2oz) caster sugar

The pears have to be poached at least 2 hours in advance to allow them to cool down in their juices; they can be poached the day before and kept in the fridge until served. The blackcurrant (cassis) coulis can be prepared up to a day in advance and kept in the fridge until served.

1. With a potato peeler, peel the pears very carefully, leaving the stalk on and not marking the fruit too deeply. Set aside. In an 18cm (7in) stainless steel pan, bring the water, caster sugar and vanilla pod to the boil. Place the peeled pears and lemon juice into the pan and cover with an 18cm (7in) disc of greaseproof paper. Bring back to the boil and simmer for 4–6 minutes. Remove the pan from the heat and leave the pears to cool in the cooking juices for about 2 hours or until they are at room temperature. Set aside in the fridge if you are not serving the pears immediately.

2. To prepare the blackcurrant coulis, bring the water to the boil in a large pan. Put 200g (7oz) of the blackcurrants into the boiling water for about 20 seconds, then drain through a sieve. Place the partly cooked blackcurrants into a liquidiser or food processor and liquidise. Pass through a sieve into a bowl, pressing as much as you can out of the purée. Stir in the sugar and if the purée is too thick, loosen with a little water.

3. Drain the pears from their cooking juices. If you like, using a Parisian scoop, you can very carefully remove the core from each pear. Trim the wide bottom of each pear slightly to allow them to stand up. Place each one in the centre of a plate. In a small container, place 2 tablespoons of the blackcurrant coulis and the remaining fresh blackcurrants. Mix gently to coat the blackcurrants. Pour the remaining blackcurrant coulis equally around each pear, then sprinkle around the coated fresh blackcurrants, and serve.

Ainsley Harriott's

APPLE MAPLE PANCAKES WITH BLACKBERRY COMPOTE

MAKES
18–20

INGREDIENTS

2 red-skinned eating apples
1 tbsp maple syrup
½ tsp ground cinnamon
2 tsp butter
150g (5oz) plain flour
½ tsp baking powder
pinch of salt
50g (2oz) caster sugar
175ml (6fl oz) milk
2 large eggs, separated
maple syrup, to serve

FOR THE BLACKBERRY COMPOTE
300g (11oz) blackberries
1 tbsp caster sugar

It's such a shame that for many of us the only time we turn our hands to making pancakes is on Shrove Tuesday, because they are among the simplest and most satisfying things to make.

1. Make the compote first. Place the blackberries in a small pan, add the sugar and cook over a low heat until tender and juicy. Remove from the heat. Core but do not peel the apples, then slice into rings no thicker than a £1 coin. You will need at least 18–20 slices. Place them in a bowl, add the maple syrup and cinnamon and mix to coat.

2. Melt half the butter in a large frying pan set over a medium heat. Add half the sliced apples and cook for 30–60 seconds, until starting to soften. Remove from the pan and cook the remaining apple slices. Wash and dry the frying pan.

3. Sift the flour, baking powder and salt into a medium-sized bowl. Add the sugar and mix to combine. In a jug whisk together the milk and the egg yolks. Pour this into the dry ingredients and mix to make a smooth batter. In a clean bowl whisk the egg whites until they will just stand in stiff peaks. Gently fold into the batter.

4. Lightly grease the pan with a little of the remaining butter and place over a medium heat. Arrange four apple slices in the pan, 4–5cm (1½–2in) apart and spoon 1 tablespoon of batter over each slice. Cook until small bubbles appear on the surface of the pancakes and their undersides are golden brown. Flip the pancakes over with a palette knife and cook for a further minute. Transfer to a plate and keep warm while you cook the remaining pancakes in the same way. You may need to wipe the pan clean with kitchen paper after each batch.

5. Serve the warm pancakes with the blackberry compote spooned over and a generous glug of maple syrup.

Gizzi Erskine's

STICKY BANOFFEE PUDDING

SERVES
6

INGREDIENTS

250g (9oz) dates, stoned and chopped
250ml (8fl oz) hot black tea, made with
   1 teabag
1 tsp bicarbonate of soda
85g (3½oz) unsalted butter, softened, plus
   extra for greasing
175g (6oz) caster sugar
2 large eggs, beaten
175g (6oz) self-raising flour, sieved
3 bananas, roughly mashed
1 tsp ground mixed spice
vanilla ice cream, or clotted cream, to
   serve

FOR THE SAUCE

100g (4oz) light muscovado sugar
100g (4oz) unsalted butter
150ml (5fl oz) double cream

The banana in this recipe is terrific with the toffeeish dates and keeps the pudding really moist. Remove the bananas and you've got a classic sticky toffee pudding.

1. Preheat the oven to 180°C/350°F/gas 4 and butter the baking dish. Place the dates in a small pan and cover with the hot tea. Bring to the boil and cook for 3–4 minutes, until the dates have softened, then stir in the bicarbonate of soda.

2. Cream together the butter and sugar until light and fluffy, then add the beaten eggs gradually. Fold in the flour, bananas, mixed spice and the date mixture, then pour into the baking dish. Bake for 30–35 minutes, until the top is springy and a skewer comes out clean when inserted into the centre.

3. While the pudding is cooking, make the sauce. Put the muscovado sugar, butter and cream into a pan, place over a low heat and melt until the sugar has dissolved. Increase the heat and simmer for 3–4 minutes, or until the sauce is a light toffee colour. Serve the pudding with the warm sauce and a big scoop of vanilla ice cream or clotted cream.

EQUIPMENT NEEDED: a 23cm (9in) baking dish

PASSION SPONGE

SERVES
4–6

INGREDIENTS

1 × 18–20cm (7–8in) ready-made sponge
  flan case
1 × 400g (14oz) tin raspberries in natural
  juice
framboise or cassis liqueur (optional)
150ml (5fl oz) double cream (not extra
  thick)
225g (8oz) Greek yoghurt
1–2 tbsp light soft brown sugar
100g (4oz) fresh raspberries, to decorate

This is a variation of my ever-popular passion pudding. It takes all of 5 minutes to make.

1. Place the sponge flan case on a serving plate. Drain the raspberries, saving the juice, and spoon them evenly over the flan case. Spoon over a little of the reserved juice with a splash of the liqueur (if using).

2. Whisk the double cream until stiff, then fold in the Greek yoghurt. Pile it on top of the raspberries.

3. Sprinkle over the sugar and chill in the fridge until the sugar has melted into the topping. Decorate with fresh raspberries just before serving.

Ainsley Harriott's

CHILLI-GLAZED MANGO WITH MINTED YOGHURT

SERVES
4

INGREDIENTS

285g (9½oz) Greek yoghurt
1 tbsp chopped fresh mint
2 large mangoes, peeled and flesh cut
 away from the stone
50g (2oz) butter
25g (1oz) icing sugar
¼ tsp hot chilli powder

The combination of flavours in this dessert will revive even the most jaded of palates. You'll need roughly 550g (1¼lb) of mango chunks in total.

1. Preheat the grill. Place the yoghurt in a serving bowl and mix in the mint. Cut the mango flesh into large chunks.

2. Melt the butter in a small pan or in the microwave. Place the mango in a large bowl and pour over the melted butter, tossing to coat evenly.

3. Line the grill rack with foil and arrange the buttered mango on top in an even layer. Sift the icing sugar and chilli powder into a small bowl, then tip into an icing-sugar duster or sieve. Sprinkle over the mango and then cook for 8–10 minutes, turning occasionally, until the mango is heated through and has caramelised.

4. Leave the mango pieces to 'set' for about 5 minutes, then serve with the minted yoghurt.

Raymond Blanc's

CHERRY CLAFOUTIS

INGREDIENTS

500g (1lb 2oz) fresh cherries, stoned
5 tbsp caster sugar, plus extra to sprinkle
2 tbsp kirsch (optional)
10g (¼oz) unsalted butter, melted

FOR THE BATTER
100g (4oz) plain white flour
a pinch of salt
3 eggs plus 1 egg yolk
6 tbsp caster sugar
finely grated zest of 1 lemon
6 drops of natural vanilla extract (optional)
150ml (5fl oz) milk
150ml (5fl oz) whipping cream
75g (3oz) unsalted butter

Clafoutis is a great family dish. Everyone should know how to make this dessert. It is so easy to prepare and your children, husband, wife and friends will love you two thousand times more for it. Put the clafoutis in the oven just before you sit down to eat your meal, then it will be at the right temperature when you serve it; just warm is best.

1. Mix the cherries with 2 tablespoons of the caster sugar and the kirsch (if using) and leave for 2 hours to maximise their flavour.

2. Brush the inside of the baking dish with the melted butter. Sprinkle in the remaining 3 tablespoons of caster sugar and shake the dish so it coats the inside evenly. This will give the clafoutis a lovely crust during cooking. Preheat the oven to 180°C/350°F/gas 4.

3. To make the batter, put the flour and salt in a mixing bowl and make a well in the centre. Add the eggs, egg yolk, sugar, lemon zest and the vanilla (if using). With a whisk, slowly incorporate the egg mixture into the flour until smooth. Whisk in the milk and cream. In a small pan, heat the butter until it turns a pale hazelnut colour, then whisk it into the batter while still hot.

4. Mix the cherries and their juices into the batter and then pour into the baking dish. Bake for 30–35 minutes, until the blade of a knife inserted into the mixture comes out completely clean. Sprinkle a little caster sugar over and serve warm.

EQUIPMENT NEEDED: a round or oval cast-iron or china baking dish, 20cm (8in) in diameter and 5cm (2in) deep

Gizzi Erskine's
BAILEYS CHOCOLATE CROISSANT BUTTER PUDDING

SERVES
6

INGREDIENTS

50g (2oz) golden caster sugar
1 large egg, plus 5 yolks
300ml (10fl oz) Baileys Irish Cream liqueur
400ml (14fl oz) double cream
butter, for greasing
6–8 chocolate croissants, torn into pieces
75g (3oz) light muscovado sugar

FOR THE BUTTERSCOTCH SAUCE
100g (4oz) light muscovado sugar
100g (4oz) butter
150ml (5fl oz) double cream

I came across a similar recipe to this while working at BBC *Good Food*. It was a pivotal point in my pudding-making career, as I had never before tasted anything quite so amazing. I have made it my own by adding even more booze to the custard and simply making it really gooey. Be warned: it is one of those puddings that has you believing that you can eat the whole lot.

1. Preheat the oven to 200°C/400°F/gas 6. In a bowl, whisk together the caster sugar, whole egg and egg yolks. Put the Baileys and double cream into a pan and bring to the boil. Whisk this into the egg mixture, then leave to cool slightly into a custard.

2. Lightly grease the baking dish with butter. Place a layer of croissant pieces in the base and add a generous sprinkle of muscovado sugar and a little of the egg custard. Keep on layering croissants, sugar and custard in the same way, finishing off with a sprinkling of sugar. Let the pudding sit for 10 minutes so it soaks up all the custard.

3. Bake for 18–20 minutes, until the pudding is puffed up, golden and crisp (the muscovado sugar will give a tasty and sticky finish). Meanwhile, make the sauce. Place the sugar and butter in a pan and stir over a medium heat until the sugar has dissolved. Pour in the cream and bring to the boil. Reduce the heat and simmer for 3–4 minutes, until dark and sticky. To serve, scoop out servings of the pudding and pour over a little of the warm sauce.

EQUIPMENT NEEDED: a 30 × 20cm (12 × 8in) baking dish

Raymond Blanc's

VANILLA ICE CREAM

INGREDIENTS

8 egg yolks
120g (4½oz) caster sugar
4 tsp dried milk
500ml (17fl oz) milk
1 vanilla pod

For this recipe you will need an ice-cream machine. It will be a very good investment as you will be able to prepare so many easy ice creams, sorbets and desserts in very little time. These are very much better than many bought versions, most of which are full of emulsifiers, additives, colourings, flavourings and far too much sugar. Maturing the cream in the fridge for 24 hours before freezing will improve both its taste and texture.

1. In a large mixing bowl, cream together the egg yolks, sugar and dried milk until a pale straw colour. Pour the milk into a heavy-based pan. Halve the vanilla pod lengthways and scrape the seeds out into the milk. Chop the pod very finely, and add to the milk as well. Bring to the boil, then simmer for about 5 minutes.

2. Bring the milk back to the boil and pour it onto the egg, sugar and dried milk mixture, whisking continuously. Return the mixture to the pan on a medium heat. Stir the custard until it thickens and coats the back of your spoon. Strain immediately through a sieve into a bowl, pressing down on the vanilla to get as much flavour as possible, then stir for a few minutes. Put the bowl into another bowl filled with ice, and cool, before churning in the ice-cream machine.

EQUIPMENT NEEDED: an ice-cream machine

Mary Berry's

LEMON MERINGUE PIE

INGREDIENTS

FOR THE BASE
175g (6oz) digestive biscuits
75g (3oz) butter

FOR THE FILLING
1 × 397g (14oz) tin full-fat condensed milk
3 large egg yolks
finely grated zest and juice of 3 lemons

FOR THE TOPPING
3 large egg whites
175g (6oz) caster sugar

EQUIPMENT NEEDED: a deep
20cm (8in) fluted flan dish

TIP: The flan dish can be lined with
the biscuit crumb mix, covered and
kept in the fridge for up to 3 days. The
filling can be mixed, covered and kept
in the fridge for up to 8 hours before
baking. Once baked, the pie can be
eaten warm or cold, but the meringue
shrinks a little on standing.

This recipe uses an easy, quick crumb crust rather than the usual
pastry base, and the filling does not have to be cooked before it
goes into the pie. You have only to stir a few ingredients together
and it is ready.

1. Preheat the oven to 190°C/375°F/gas 5.

2. Put the biscuits into a plastic bag and crush with a rolling pin.
    Melt the butter in a medium-sized pan. Remove the pan from
    the heat and stir in the biscuit crumbs. Press into the bottom
    and up the sides of the flan dish and leave to set.

3. Pour the condensed milk into a bowl, then beat in the egg
    yolks, lemon zest and strained lemon juice. The mixture
    will seem to thicken on standing, then loosen again as soon as it
    is stirred. This is caused by the combination of condensed milk
    and lemon juice and is nothing to worry about. Pour the mixture
    into the biscuit-lined dish.

4. Whisk the egg whites until stiff but not dry. Gradually add the
    the sugar, a teaspoon at a time, whisking well between each
    addition. Whisk until the meringue is very stiff and all of the
    sugar has been added.

5. Pile separate spoonfuls of meringue over the surface of the
    filling, then spread gently to cover the filling to the biscuit
    edge, lightly swirling the meringue.

6. Bake in the preheated oven for 15–20 minutes or until the
    meringue is light brown. Leave to cool for about 30 minutes
    before serving warm.

Ainsley Harriott's
ORANGE FLOWER, YOGHURT AND PISTACHIO PUDDING

INGREDIENTS

butter, for greasing
3 eggs, separated
75g (3oz) caster sugar
1 tbsp plain flour
1 tbsp orange flower water
grated zest and juice of 1 lemon
300ml (10fl oz) thick Greek yoghurt
40g (1½oz) shelled unsalted pistachios,
   roughly chopped
crème fraîche or vanilla ice cream, to serve

You just have to try this recipe for a beautiful, light pudding with a gorgeous moist base. Orange flower water is available from most large supermarkets or from specialist food stores; it has a wonderfully fragrant flavour. For an extra special touch, stir a splash of vanilla extract into some Greek yoghurt and serve with the pudding.

1. Preheat the oven to 160°C/325°F/gas 3. Butter and line the tin. Place the egg yolks and sugar in a large bowl and, using an electric beater or wooden spoon, beat until pale and fluffy. Fold in the flour, orange flower water, lemon zest and juice until well combined. Finally stir in the yoghurt and half the pistachio nuts.

2. Whisk the egg whites in a separate large bowl until stiff peaks form. Stir 1 spoonful of beaten egg whites into the yoghurt mixture to loosen it, then gently fold in the remaining egg white, being careful not to knock out too much air.

3. Spoon the mixture into the prepared cake tin and bake for 20 minutes. Remove from the oven, sprinkle the remaining pistachio nuts over the top, increase the heat to 180°C/350°F/ gas 4 and cook for a further 15 minutes until the pudding has risen and is golden brown.

4. Remove the pudding from the oven and leave to cool for about 5 minutes – don't worry if it sinks slightly, as that's supposed to happen. Spoon the warm pudding onto plates, and serve with a dollop of crème fraîche or vanilla ice cream.

CAKE TIN NEEDED: a 23cm (9in) spring-form cake tin

Raymond Blanc's

CHOCOLATE MOUSSE

SERVES
4

INGREDIENTS

165g (5½oz) dark chocolate, at least
   70 per cent cocoa solids, finely chopped
25g (1oz) unsweetened cocoa powder
10 egg whites, plus 1 egg yolk
25g (1oz) caster sugar
fresh mint sprigs, to decorate

Do use the very best chocolate, with 70 per cent cocoa solids, and also the very best unsweetened cocoa powder for this simple but delicious chocolate mousse recipe.

1. Place the chocolate and cocoa powder in a large bowl set over a pan of hot water and leave to melt over a low heat; do not boil the water or the chocolate will become grainy. Stir until smooth, then remove from the heat. Keep warm over the pan of water.

2. With an electric beater, whisk the egg whites and sugar for 2–3 minutes, until they form soft peaks. Stir the egg yolk into the chocolate and cocoa mixture, and immediately whisk in a quarter of the egg whites to lighten the mixture. Fold in the remaining egg whites with a large spatula, ensuring that you do not over mix or the mousse will be heavy.

3. Pour into a glass bowl or individual glasses and leave to set in the fridge for 2 hours or until required. Garnish with a sprig of fresh mint before serving.

Gizzi Erskine's

LEMON AND PASSION FRUIT
SELF-SAUCING PUDDING

SERVES
4–6

INGREDIENTS

50g (2oz) butter, plus extra for greasing
150g (5oz) caster sugar
juice and zest of 1 lemon
120ml (4fl oz) passion fruit juice (if making
   it yourself, use about 16 passion fruits)
3 large eggs, separated
50g (2oz) plain flour, sifted
250ml (8fl oz) milk

TO SERVE
cream
fresh raspberries

My mum makes the most amazing pudding called lemon surprise tart, which is a crisp pastry tart with gooey lemon sponge in the centre. It is so calorific, though, that I wanted to see if I could make it a little kinder on the waistline. By ditching the crust, you end up with a self-saucing sponge pudding that leaves a wicked custardy curd at the bottom. With the addition of passion fruit, this makes a really light end to your meal, and it's great for Sunday lunch after a heavy roast.

1. Preheat the oven to 160°C/325°F/gas 3 and grease a baking dish. In a food processor, whizz together the butter, sugar and lemon zest until pale and creamy. One ingredient at a time, add the lemon juice, passion fruit juice, egg yolks, flour and milk until you have a smooth batter. Whisk the egg whites until firm but not stiff and fold them into the batter.

2. Pour the batter into the baking dish and place in a baking tray. Half-fill the baking tray with hot water (to make a bain-marie). Put this in the oven and bake for 45–50 minutes, until the top is lightly browned and set and there is a sort of gooey curd below. Remove the dish from the tray and serve hot, with cream and raspberries.

Ainsley Harriott's

CHEAT'S BANOFFEE PIE WITH CHOCOLATE DRIZZLE

SERVES
6

INGREDIENTS

vegetable oil, for greasing
225g (8oz) digestive biscuits
100g (4oz) butter
1 × 450g (1lb) jar banoffee toffee sauce
2 large ripe bananas, peeled and sliced
450ml (15fl oz) double cream
¾ tsp instant coffee powder
1 tbsp caster sugar
25g (1oz) plain or milk chocolate, melted,
    to serve

Traditionally this pie is made in a pastry case and calls for boiling an unopened tin of condensed milk in a deep pan of water for 5 hours. But the good news is that you can now buy banoffee toffee sauce ready made in jars. If you can't find it, drizzle some toffee ice-cream sauce over the bananas instead.

1. Lightly oil the flan tin. Put the biscuits into a plastic bag and crush into fine crumbs using a rolling pin. Melt the butter in a medium-sized pan and stir in the crushed biscuits. Press the mixture onto the base and sides of the prepared flan tin. Chill for 15 minutes.

2. Spread the banoffee toffee sauce over the base of the biscuit case and cover with the sliced bananas.

3. In a bowl lightly whip together the cream, instant coffee and caster sugar until the mixture just forms soft peaks. Spoon this on top of the bananas and spread it out to make a seal with the edge of the biscuit case. Swirl the top attractively and chill for at least 1 hour.

4. To serve, carefully remove the pie from the tin, drizzle with the warm melted chocolate and cut into wedges.

EQUIPMENT NEEDED: a 23cm (9in) loose-bottomed flan tin that is 4cm (1½in) deep

PINEAPPLE AND GINGER FOOL

INGREDIENTS

1 × 400g (14oz) tin crushed pineapple,
   drained
4 pieces stem ginger, drained and
   chopped
450ml (15fl oz) Greek yoghurt
toasted almond flakes, to sprinkle
4 fresh mint sprigs, to decorate

This is simplicity itself. Serve in attractive glasses or a large serving dish.

1. Mix together the crushed pineapple, stem ginger and Greek yoghurt.

2. Pour into glasses or a large bowl and chill thoroughly before serving, sprinkled with almonds and decorated with sprigs of fresh mint.

Ainsley Harriott's
QUICK BLUEBERRY, LEMON AND CRÈME FRAÎCHE CHEESECAKE

SERVES
8

INGREDIENTS

2 large lemons
225g (8oz) full-fat cream cheese
100g (4oz) caster sugar
200g (7oz) crème fraîche

FOR THE BASE

100g (4oz) butter
225g (8oz) digestive biscuits
1½ tbsp demerara sugar
oil, for greasing

FOR THE BLUEBERRY TOPPING

3 tbsp lemon juice
50g (2oz) caster sugar
150g (5oz) blueberries
1 tsp arrowroot

EQUIPMENT NEEDED: a 20cm (8in) loose-bottomed flan tin

This cheesecake is extra easy because it does not require any gelatine. The action of the lemon juice on the cream cheese and crème fraîche helps it set all on its own.

1. To make the base, put the butter into a large pan and melt over a low heat. Put the biscuits into a large plastic bag, seal the end and crush with a rolling pin into fine crumbs. Stir into the butter, along with the demerara sugar. Lightly oil the flan tin, then press the mixture firmly onto the base and sides of the prepared flan tin using the back of a spoon. Chill while you make the filling.

2. Finely grate the zest from one lemon and squeeze the juice from both – you should get 150ml (5fl oz) of juice. In a bowl beat together the cream cheese, sugar and lemon zest until smooth. Very gradually, beat in the lemon juice until you have a thick, creamy mixture, then gently fold in the crème fraîche. Spoon the filling into the biscuit case, swirl the top with a knife and chill for at least 2 hours.

3. To make the topping, put the lemon juice and sugar into a small pan and leave over a low heat until the sugar has dissolved. Add the blueberries, bring to a gentle simmer and cook for 1 minute. Mix the arrowroot with 1 teaspoon of cold water, stir in and cook for about 30 seconds until thickened. Transfer to a bowl and leave to cool. Then cover and chill alongside the cheesecake.

4. Remove the cheesecake from the flan tin and transfer it to a serving plate. Spoon over the blueberry topping, cut into wedges and serve.

JAMAICAN STICKY
TOFFEE PUDDING

INGREDIENTS

2 × 275g (10oz) Jamaican ginger cakes
50g (2oz) butter
100g (4oz) light muscovado sugar
120ml (4fl oz) pouring golden syrup
150ml (5fl oz) double cream, plus extra for
   serving (optional)

An all-time favourite in our house, this pudding also works with Madeira cake, chocolate marble cake or even banana bread.

1. Preheat the oven to 180°C/350°F/gas 4. Cut each ginger cake into 8 slices. Select an ovenproof dish that's big enough to accommodate all the slices and arrange them inside in a slightly overlapping layer.

2. Place the butter in a pan along with the sugar and golden syrup. Bring to the boil, then reduce the heat and simmer for a minute or two, stirring occasionally, until the sugar has dissolved and a bubbling and lightly golden caramel has formed. Mix the cream into the caramel and simmer for a further few minutes, stirring occasionally, until you have a toffee sauce.

3. Pour the toffee sauce over the cake slices and bake for 15–20 minutes until bubbling. Serve straight to the table, with more cream, if you like.

Gizzi Erskine's
ETON MESS WITH LEMON CURD, PASSION FRUIT AND RASPBERRIES

INGREDIENTS

300ml (10fl oz) double cream

1 tbsp icing sugar

a few drops of vanilla extract

4 large ready-made meringues, broken up

5 tbsp good-quality ready-made lemon curd

150g (5 oz) fresh raspberries

2 passion fruits, pulped

Eton mess has to be one of the most brilliant desserts ever. It's light, it has texture and it's super more-ish. Traditionally, it's served with berries, but I've given it a bit of a twist by using lemon curd and passion fruits too.

1. Whisk together the double cream, icing sugar and vanilla extract until it becomes thick, but is still able to leave a trail. Don't over whip it and make it foamy as it will begin to taste a little buttery, or sometimes even cheesy!

2. Add the broken-up meringues, lemon curd and raspberries to the mixture and give it all a good mix. The gentler you do it, the more obvious the marble effect of the lemon curd running through it will be. Divide among four plates, then top each plate with some of the passion fruit pulp.

Raymond Blanc's

STRAWBERRY SORBET

INGREDIENTS

450g (1lb) ripe fresh strawberries
80g (3¼oz) caster sugar
a dash of lemon juice

Only use the sweetest seasonal strawberries for this recipe. I always look forward to the first Gaurigette strawberries in France, while we wait for the British strawberries to ripen enough to be picked. This recipe can be adapted to any soft berries, but always taste your fruit and adjust the sugar according to the sweetness.

1. Wash the fruit briefly under cold running water while the stems are still in place. Drain and dry on kitchen paper. Pull or cut off the stems, then slice the fruit. Place in a bowl and sprinkle with the caster sugar and lemon juice. Mix and leave to marinate for 30 minutes at room temperature.

2. Liquidise the strawberry mixture and pass it through a fine sieve. Place in the ice-cream machine and churn until frozen. Keep in the freezer until ready to serve.

EQUIPMENT NEEDED: an ice-cream machine

Ainsley Harriott's
CHOCOLATE FRUIT AND NUT FRIDGE CAKE

SERVES
6–8

INGREDIENTS

350g (12oz) plain chocolate

75g (3oz) unsalted butter

2 tbsp clear honey

1 large egg, beaten

250g (9oz) mixed dried fruit, such as glacé cherries, ready-to-eat apricots, sultanas and raisins

100g (4oz) toasted nuts, such as hazelnuts and almonds

100g (4oz) ginger biscuits

CAKE TIN NEEDED: a 20cm (8in) cake tin or small roasting tin

TIP: I've used ginger biscuits here, but the recipe would easily work with digestives or oaty biscuits. To make it fancier, add a little chopped stem ginger or finely chopped candied peel.

As my old pastry chef Aldo would say, 'Respect the cioccolato, it's a beautiful thing'. This recipe is very versatile because you can use a mixture of whatever dried fruit and nuts you have to hand. If you're making the cake for the children, think about using chocolate with a lower cocoa fat content.

1. Line the tin with baking parchment or clingfilm. Break the chocolate into chunks into a heatproof bowl and melt gently, either in a microwave or over a pan of simmering water. (Don't let the bowl touch the water – just let the hot steam melt it.) When nice and smooth, mix in the butter and honey, stirring until melted and thoroughly combined. Slowly beat in the egg for a good minute, then remove from the heat.

2. Halve the cherries and roughly chop the apricots and nuts. Tip the biscuits into a plastic bag and bash a couple of times with a rolling pin to break them into smallish pieces, not crumbs. Add the nuts, dried fruit and biscuits to the melted chocolate mixture and fold in thoroughly.

3. Spoon into the prepared tin, level out with a spatula and leave to cool. When cold, cover lightly with clingfilm and chill until set – normally 3–4 hours.

4. Peel off the clingfilm and cut into small squares.

Mary Berry's

GUERNSEY APPLE CAKE

INGREDIENTS

225g (8oz) self-raising brown flour
grated zest of 1 lemon
1 level tsp baking powder
100g (4oz) butter, plus extra for greasing
225g (8oz) light muscovado sugar
2 large eggs
175g (6oz) apples, peeled, cored and
   chopped
icing sugar, for dusting

A wonderful way to use up some apples if you have a glut, this is best served warm with whipped cream. Expect it to dip a little in the middle.

1. Preheat the oven to 160°C/325°F/gas 6. Butter the tin, then line the base with non-stick baking parchment.

2. Measure the flour, lemon zest, baking powder, butter, sugar and eggs into a bowl and mix together until evenly blended and smooth. Fold in the chopped apples.

3. Spoon the mixture into the prepared tin and bake for 1–1¼ hours or until well risen and the surface springs back when lightly pressed in the centre with a finger.

4. Allow to cool in the tin for about 10 minutes before turning out to cool completely on a wire rack. Dust with icing sugar and eat within 1–2 days.

CAKE TIN NEEDED: a deep, round 18cm (7in) cake tin

Mary Berry's
AMERICAN SPICED CARROT TRAYBAKE

MAKES
16
PIECES

INGREDIENTS

butter, for greasing
275g (10oz) self-raising flour
350g (12oz) caster sugar
2 level tsp baking powder
75g (3oz) chopped unsalted mixed nuts
3 level tsp ground cinnamon
2 level tsp ground ginger
300ml (10fl oz) sunflower oil
275g (10oz) grated carrots
4 large eggs
1 tsp vanilla extract

FOR THE TOPPING
400g (14oz) full-fat soft cheese
4 tsp clear honey
2 tsp lemon juice
very finely chopped mixed unsalted nuts,
   to decorate

Bought mixtures of chopped nuts might include a high proportion of peanuts. I always prefer to make up my own mix from shelled nuts.

1. Preheat the oven to 180°C/350°F/gas 4. Butter the tin, then line the base with non-stick baking parchment.

2. Measure all the dry cake ingredients into a large bowl. Add the oil, grated carrots, eggs (one at a time) and vanilla extract, beating between each addition. Pour into the prepared tin and level the surface.

3. Bake in the preheated oven for 50–60 minutes or until the cake is well risen, golden brown in colour and firm to the touch. Leave to cool in the tin for 10 minutes, then turn out, peel off the parchment and finish cooling on a wire rack.

4. To make the topping, mix together the cheese, honey and lemon juice, adding, if necessary, a little extra lemon juice to make a spreading consistency. Spread evenly over the cake with a palette knife, then sprinkle over the very finely chopped nuts to decorate and cut into 16 pieces. You can store the iced cake in the fridge for up to 2 weeks.

CAKE TIN NEEDED: a 30 × 23cm (12 × 9in) traybake or roasting tin

Mary Berry's

SPICED CHERRY ROCK CAKES

INGREDIENTS

225g (8oz) self-raising flour

2 level tsp baking powder

100g (4oz) butter, softened, plus extra
for greasing

50g (2oz) sugar

150g (5oz) glacé cherries, rinsed, dried
and quartered

1 level tsp ground mixed spice

1 large egg

about 1 tbsp milk

demerara sugar, for sprinkling

These are very traditional English cakes, but this version is slightly different, with the addition of cherries and spice. They're inexpensive, can be large or tiny, and need no special equipment. They are best eaten on the day of making.

1. Preheat the oven to 200°C/400°F/gas 6. Lightly butter the baking trays.

2. Measure the flour and baking powder into a large bowl, add the butter and rub in with your fingertips until the mixture resembles fine breadcrumbs. Stir in the sugar, cherries and spice.

3. Beat the egg and milk together and add to the fruity mixture. If the mixture is too dry, add a little more milk. Using a pair of teaspoons, shape the mixture into about 12 rough mounds and place on the prepared baking trays. Sprinkle generously with demerara sugar.

4. Bake in the preheated oven for about 15 minutes or until a pale golden brown at the edges. Cool on a wire rack.

EQUIPMENT NEEDED: 2 baking trays

TIP: Use wholemeal self-raising flour, if you like, although you may need to add a little more milk to the mix.

Mary Berry's

BAKEWELL SLICES

MAKES
24
PIECES

INGREDIENTS

FOR THE SHORTCRUST PASTRY
175g (6oz) plain flour
75g (3oz) butter

FOR THE SPONGE MIXTURE
100g (4oz) butter, softened
100g (4oz) caster sugar
175g (6oz) self-raising flour
1 level tsp baking powder
2 large eggs
2 tbsp milk
½ tsp almond extract

TO FINISH
about 4 tbsp raspberry jam
flaked almonds, for sprinkling

Be generous with the raspberry jam – it makes all the difference. As the shortcrust pastry contains a lot of fat and no sugar, there is no need to line the tin with non-stick baking parchment.

1. To make the pastry, measure the flour into a bowl and rub in the butter with your fingertips until the mixture resembles fine breadcrumbs. Add 2–3 tablespoons cold water gradually, mixing to form a soft dough.

2. Preheat the oven to 180°C/350°F/gas 4. Roll the dough out on a lightly floured work surface and use it to line the tin.

3. Measure all the sponge ingredients into a bowl and beat until well blended. Spread the pastry with raspberry jam and then top with the sponge mixture. Sprinkle with the flaked almonds.

4. Bake in the preheated oven for about 25 minutes or until the cake has shrunk from the sides of the tin and springs back when pressed in the centre with your fingertips. Leave to cool in the tin and then cut into slices.

CAKE TIN NEEDED: a 30 × 23cm (12 × 9in) traybake or roasting tin

ICED CHOCOLATE TRAYBAKE
WITH FUDGE ICING

MAKES
21
PIECES

INGREDIENTS

4 level tbsp cocoa powder
225g (8oz) butter, softened, plus extra
    for greasing
225g (8oz) caster sugar
275g (10oz) self-raising flour
2 level tsp baking powder
4 large eggs
4 tbsp milk

FOR THE ICING AND DECORATION
4 level tbsp apricot jam
50g (2oz) butter
25g (1oz) cocoa powder, sifted
3 tbsp milk
225g (8oz) icing sugar, sifted
chocolate, for making curls, to decorate

Chocolate cakes are always popular, and this is a particularly simple version. We often serve it as a dessert by pouring the hot icing over the top.

1. Preheat the oven to 180°C/350°F/gas 4. Butter the tin, then line the base with non-stick baking parchment.

2. Blend together the cocoa powder and 4 tablespoons hot water, then allow to cool slightly. Measure all the remaining cake ingredients into a large bowl, add the cocoa mixture and beat until well blended. Turn the mixture into the prepared tin and level the surface.

3. Bake for 35–40 minutes or until the cake has shrunk from the sides of the tin and the centre of the cake springs back when pressed with your fingertips. Leave to cool in the tin.

4. Warm the apricot jam in a pan and brush all over the cake. Then melt the butter in a small pan, add the cocoa powder, stir to blend and cook gently for 1 minute. Stir in the milk and icing sugar, remove from the heat and mix very well, then leave on one side, stirring occasionally, until the icing thickens.

5. Pour over the cold cake and smooth over gently with a palette knife. Leave to set for about 30 minutes, then cut into pieces. To make the chocolate curls, let the chocolate come to room temperature and then shave using a vegetable peeler. Decorate the pieces with the chocolate curls and serve.

CAKE TIN NEEDED: a 30 × 23cm
(12 × 9in) traybake or roasting tin

 **Mary Berry's**

TOFFEE MARSHMALLOW SQUARES

INGREDIENTS

100g (4oz) butter
100g (4oz) marshmallows
100g (4oz) dairy toffees
150g (5oz) small puffed-rice cereal

I have included this recipe here because it is very popular with all children. And, with supervision, even very young ones can make them.

1. Measure the butter, marshmallows and toffees into a thick-based pan and heat gently until the mixture is melted and smooth. This will take about 5 minutes.

2. Place the small puffed-rice cereal in a bowl. Pour over the toffee mixture and stir well to mix.

3. Spoon into the tin and press flat. Leave in a cool place until quite firm and then cut into squares.

CAKE TIN NEEDED: a 30 × 23cm (12 × 9in) oblong baking tin

TIP: Be sure to use small puffed-rice cereal for this recipe. Larger puffed-rice grains absorb too much liquid.

HOT ORANGE BUNS

MAKES
6–8
BUNS

INGREDIENTS

40g (1½oz) unsalted butter, softened, plus
    extra for greasing
finely grated zest of 1 orange
finely grated zest of ½ lemon
50g (2oz) caster sugar
1 egg
1 tbsp milk
a pinch of salt
70g (2¾oz) self-raising flour
plain flour, for dusting

FOR THE BUN MOULDS
50g (2oz) unsalted butter, softened
2 tbsp plain flour

The bun mixture can be made up to a half a day in advance and kept covered in the fridge until needed.

1. In a medium bowl, cream the butter until soft. Whisk in the orange and lemon zests and the caster sugar. Add the egg, milk and a pinch of salt, and whisk again. Fold in the self-raising flour. Rest in the fridge for at least an hour.

2. Pre-heat the oven to 180°C/350°F/gas 4. With a pastry brush, coat the inside of each mould or tin generously with the soft butter and dust with the plain flour. Shake off the excess flour and place the moulds in the fridge for 15 minutes to allow the butter to set.

3. With a tablespoon, fill the prepared moulds up to the top with the bun mixture and bake for about 12 minutes until a light blond colour. The buns should have a spongy texture, and a crust should have built up underneath. Remove the cooked buns from the moulds or tin, and allow to cool a little on a wire rack. Serve while still warm.

EQUIPMENT NEEDED: 6 large 'bun' moulds, muffin moulds or cake tins, which contain about 20ml (¾fl oz) each

Mary Berry's

IRISH SODA BREAD

MAKES
1
LOAF

INGREDIENTS

oil, for greasing
450g (1lb) strong white flour
1 level tsp bicarbonate of soda
1 level tsp salt
300ml (10fl oz) buttermilk or 150ml
(5fl oz) milk and 150ml (5fl oz) natural
yoghurt, mixed

Soda bread is quick and easy to make, as it uses no yeast so does not have to rise. Porridge oats can be added to give the bread more texture. Simply replace 50g (2oz) of the flour with the same quantity of oats. Soda bread is best eaten on the day of making.

1. Preheat the oven to 200°C/400°F/gas 6. Lightly grease the tray.

2. Measure the dry ingredients into a mixing bowl. Add the buttermilk (or milk and yoghurt mixture) and enough tepid water – about 6 tablespoons – to form a very soft dough.

3. Turn the dough out onto a lightly floured work surface and shape into a neat round about 18cm (7in) in diameter. Place on the prepared baking tray and make a shallow cross in the top with a sharp knife.

4. Bake in the preheated oven for 30 minutes, then turn the bread upside-down and continue baking for 10–15 minutes or until the bread sounds hollow when tapped on the bottom. Cool on a wire rack.

EQUIPMENT NEEDED:
a baking tray

SHREWSBURY BISCUITS

INGREDIENTS

100g (4oz) butter, softened, plus extra
   for greasing
75g (3oz) caster sugar
1 large egg, separated
200g (7oz) plain flour
grated zest of 1 lemon
50g (2oz) currants
1–2 tbsp milk
caster sugar, for sprinkling

These biscuits have a delicate lemony flavour.

1. Preheat the oven to 200°C/400°F/gas 6. Lightly butter the
   baking trays.

2. Measure the butter and sugar into a bowl and cream together
   until light and fluffy. Beat in the egg yolk. Sift in the flour, add
   the grated lemon zest and mix well. Add the currants and
   enough milk to give a fairly soft dough.

3. Knead the mixture gently on a lightly floured surface and roll
   out to a thickness of 5mm (¼in). Cut into about 24 rounds
   using a 6cm (2½in) fluted cutter. Place on the prepared
   baking trays.

4. Bake in the preheated oven for 8–10 minutes. Meanwhile,
   lightly beat the egg whites. Remove the biscuits from the oven,
   brush with beaten egg white, sprinkle with a little caster sugar
   and return to the oven for a further 4–5 minutes or until pale
   golden brown. Lift onto a wire rack to cool and then store in an
   airtight container.

EQUIPMENT NEEDED: 3 baking trays

Mary Berry's

LIME LATTICE COOKIES

MAKES
16

INGREDIENTS

100g (4oz) butter, softened, plus extra
   for greasing
50g (2oz) caster sugar
150g (5oz) self-raising flour
finely grated zest of 2 limes

Use the juice of the limes in drinks, or to add a lovely flavour to whipped cream.

1. Preheat the oven to 180°C/350°F/gas 4. Lightly butter the baking trays.

2. Measure the butter and sugar into a bowl and beat together to a creamy consistency. Add the flour and grated lime zest. Bring the mixture together to form a dough. Form the dough into 16 balls the size of a walnut and place on the prepared baking trays. Flatten the balls slightly and then use a skewer to create a lattice pattern in the top of the biscuits.

3. Bake in the preheated oven for 10–15 minutes or until just beginning to turn golden. Lift onto a wire rack and leave to cool.

EQUIPMENT NEEDED: 2 baking trays

DOUBLE CHOCOLATE COOKIES

MAKES
36

INGREDIENTS

200g (7oz) plain chocolate (39 per cent cocoa solids)
50g (2oz) butter, plus extra for greasing
1 × 397g (14oz) tin full-fat condensed milk
225g (8oz) self-raising flour
65g (2½oz) milk or white chocolate buttons

Dead easy to make, these are wonderful cookies. Expect an irregular shape. They are very soft when they come out of the oven but will harden up considerably on cooling.

1. Lightly butter the baking trays. Break up the chocolate and gently melt it along with the butter in a heatproof bowl set over a pan of barely simmering water or in a microwave, taking care not to burn the chocolate, stirring occasionally. Stir in the condensed milk, then remove from the heat and cool.

2. Mix in the flour and the chocolate buttons and chill the mixture until firm enough to handle. Preheat the oven to 180°C/350°F/gas 4.

3. Place large teaspoonfuls of the mixture spaced well apart on the prepared baking trays. Bake in the preheated oven for about 15 minutes. The cookies should still look soft and will glisten. Don't overcook them, as they soon become very hard. Carefully remove the cookies with a palette knife and cool on a wire rack.

EQUIPMENT NEEDED: 3 baking trays

BISHOP'S FINGERS

INGREDIENTS

100g (4oz) plain flour
25g (1oz) ground almonds
25g (1oz) semolina
100g (4oz) butter, plus extra
  for greasing
50g (2oz) caster sugar
a few drops almond extract
25g (1oz) flaked almonds
caster sugar, for sprinkling

If you notice that the underside of the shortbread is not pale golden, return the tin to the oven for a further 5–10 minutes.

1. Preheat the oven to 160°C/325°F/gas 3. Lightly butter the tin.

2. Mix together the flour, ground almonds and semolina in a bowl or food processor. Add the butter, sugar and almond extract and rub together with your fingertips until the mixture is just beginning to bind together. Knead lightly until smooth. Press the dough into the prepared tin and level the surface with the back of a metal spoon or a palette knife. Sprinkle over the flaked almonds.

3. Bake in the preheated oven for 30–35 minutes or until a very pale golden brown. Mark the shortbread into 12 fingers with a knife, sprinkle with caster sugar and leave to cool in the tin. When completely cold, cut into fingers, lift out carefully and store in an airtight tin.

CAKE TIN NEEDED: an 18cm (7in) shallow square tin

LAVENDER BISCUITS

INGREDIENTS

175g (6oz) unsalted butter, softened, plus extra for greasing

2 level tbsp fresh, unsprayed, finely chopped lavender flowers and leaves (pick the flowerlets and the leaves off the stems to measure), or 1 level tbsp dried lavender, plus extra, to decorate (optional)

100g (4oz) caster sugar

225g (8oz) plain flour

25g (1oz) demerara sugar

Both the flowers and the leaves of lavender can be used, although it is best to use young leaves. If you are using fresh lavender, make sure it is unsprayed. Dried lavender is stronger in flavour, so use half the quantity.

1. Lightly butter the baking trays. Put the softened butter and the lavender into a mixing bowl and beat together. This will extract the maximum flavour from the lavender.

2. Beat the caster sugar into the butter and lavender and then stir in the flour, bringing the mixture together with your hands and kneading lightly until smooth.

3. Divide the mixture in half and roll out to form two sausage shapes 15cm (6in) long. Roll the biscuit 'sausages' in the demerara sugar until evenly coated. Wrap in non-stick baking parchment or foil and chill until firm.

4. Preheat the oven to 160°C/325°F/gas 3. Cut each 'sausage' into about 10 slices and put them on the prepared baking trays, allowing a little room for them to spread. Bake in the preheated oven for 15–20 minutes, until the biscuits are pale golden brown at the edges. Lift them off the trays with a fish slice or palette knife and place on a wire rack. Sprinkle with extra lavender flowers to decorate (if using), and leave to cool completely.

EQUIPMENT NEEDED: 3 large baking trays

Mary Berry's

YORKSHIRE GINGERNUTS

INGREDIENTS

100g (4oz) butter, plus extra
   for greasing
1 generous tbsp golden syrup
350g (12oz) self-raising flour
100g (4oz) demerara sugar
100g (4oz) light muscovado sugar
1 level tsp bicarbonate of soda
1 level tbsp ground ginger
1 large egg, beaten

Very quick to make and deliciously crunchy, these biscuits look nice stored in an attractive glass jar.

1. Preheat the oven to 160°C/325°F/gas 3. Lightly butter the baking trays.

2. Measure the butter and golden syrup into a small pan and gently heat together until the butter has melted. Mix all the dry ingredients together in a large bowl, then add the melted butter mixture and the egg to form a dough.

3. Form the dough into 50 balls about the size of a walnut and place spaced well apart on the prepared baking trays.

4. Bake in the preheated oven for 15–20 minutes or until golden. Lift off the baking trays and leave to cool on a wire rack.

EQUIPMENT NEEDED: 3 baking trays

ANZAC BISCUITS

INGREDIENTS

150g (5oz) butter, softened, plus extra
  for greasing
1 tbsp golden syrup
175g (6oz) sugar
75g (3oz) self-raising flour
75g (3oz) desiccated coconut
100g (4oz) porridge oats

Also known as Diggers, these traditional Australian biscuits are really easy to make.

1. Preheat the oven to 180°C/350°F/gas 4. Lightly butter the baking trays.

2. Measure the butter, golden syrup and sugar into a medium pan and heat gently until the butter has melted and the sugar has dissolved. Stir in the flour, coconut and oats and mix well until evenly blended.

3. Place large teaspoonfuls of the mixture spaced well apart on the prepared baking trays and flatten slightly with the back of the spoon. You should have enough mixture for about 45 mounds, and you will need to bake them in batches.

4. Bake in the preheated oven for 8–10 minutes or until they have spread out flat and are lightly browned at the edges. Leave to cool on the trays for a few minutes, then carefully lift off with a palette knife and place on a wire rack to cool completely. If the biscuits harden too much to lift off the tray, pop them back in the oven for a few minutes to soften. Store in an airtight container.

EQUIPMENT NEEDED: 2 baking trays

Mary Berry's
CHOCOLATE CHIP BROWNIES

MAKES
24
PIECES

INGREDIENTS

275g (10oz) butter, softened, plus extra
  for greasing
375g (13oz) caster sugar
4 large eggs
75g (3oz) cocoa powder
100g (4oz) self-raising flour
100g (4oz) plain chocolate chips

A really simple brownie recipe – just measure all the ingredients into a bowl and give it a good mix! Be careful not to overcook your brownies: they should have a slightly gooey texture. The outside crust should be on the crisp side, though, thanks to the high proportion of sugar.

1. Preheat the oven to 180°C/350°F/gas 4. Butter the tin, then line the base and sides with non-stick baking parchment.

2. Measure all the ingredients into a large bowl and beat until evenly blended. Spoon the mixture into the prepared tin, scraping the sides of the bowl with a plastic spatula to remove all of it. Spread the mixture gently to the corners of the tin and level the top with the back of the spatula.

3. Bake in the preheated oven for 40–45 minutes or until the brownies have a crusty top and a skewer inserted into the centre comes out clean. Cover loosely with foil for the last 10 minutes if the mixture is browning too much. Leave the brownies to cool in the tin and then cut into 24 squares. Store in an airtight tin.

CAKE TIN NEEDED: a 30 × 23cm
(12 × 9in) traybake or roasting tin

INDEX

Learn to cook fantastic meals with your favourite chefs, including **Mary Berry, Rick Stein, Gizzi Erskine, Ken Hom, Antonio Carluccio** and many more.

Our Penguin Random House cookery authors will teach you how to cook meals for every occasion, from quick, light bites, to dinners designed to dazzle your guests, as well as healthy and delicious meals for the whole family to enjoy.

The My Kitchen Table series is published by Ebury Press and is available from all good bookstores.